SERENDIPITY

Serendipity – the relationship between good fortune and the prepared mind – is an appealing concept, and one which has been surprisingly influential in a great number of areas of human discovery. The essays collected in this volume provide insightful and entertaining accounts of the relationship between serendipity and knowledge in the human and natural sciences. Written by some of the most eminent thinkers of this generation, *Serendipity* explores a variety of subjects, including disease, politics, scientific invention and the art of writing. This collection will fascinate and inspire a wide range of readers, highlighting the multifaceted nature of the popular, but elusive, concept of serendipity.

THE DARWIN COLLEGE LECTURES

These essays are developed from the 2008 Darwin College Lecture Series. Now in their twenty-fifth year, these popular Cambridge talks take a single theme each year. Internationally distinguished scholars, skilled as popularizers, address the theme from the point of view of eight different arts and sciences disciplines.

Subjects covered in the series include:

23 DARWIN
eds. William Brown and Andrew Fabian
pb 9780521131957

22 SERENDIPITY
eds. Mark de Rond and Iain Morley
pb 9780521181815

21 IDENTITY
eds. Giselle Walker and Elizabeth Leedham-Green
pb 9780521897266

20 SURVIVAL
ed. Emily Shuckburgh
pb 9780521718206

19 CONFLICT
eds. Martin Jones and Andrew Fabian
hb 9780521839600

18 EVIDENCE
eds. Andrew Bell, John Swenson-Wright and Karin Tybjerg
pb 9780521710190

17 DNA: CHANGING SCIENCE AND SOCIETY
ed. Torsten Krude
hb 9780521823784

16 POWER
eds. Alan Blackwell and David Mackay
hb 9780521823717

15 SPACE
eds. François Penz, Gregory Radick and Robert Howell
hb 9780521823760

14 TIME
ed. Katinka Ridderbos
hb 9780521782937

13 THE BODY
  eds. Sean Sweeney and Ian Hodder
  hb 9780521782920

12 STRUCTURE
  eds. Wendy Pullan and Harshad Bhadeshia
  hb 9780521782586

11 SOUND
  eds. Patricia Kruth and Henry Stobart
  pb 9780521033831

10 MEMORY
  eds. Patricia Fara and Karalyn Patterson
  pb 9780521032186

9 EVOLUTION
  ed. Andrew Fabian
  pb 9780521032179

8 THE CHANGING WORLD
  eds. Patricia Fara, Peter Gathercole and Ronald Laskey
  unavailable

7 COLOUR: ART AND SCIENCE
  eds. Trevor Lamb and Janine Bourriau
  unavailable

6 WHAT IS INTELLIGENCE?
  ed. Jean Khalfa
  pb 9780521566858

5 PREDICTING THE FUTURE
  ed. Leo Howe and Alan Wain
  pb 9780521619745

4 UNDERSTANDING CATASTROPHE
  ed. Janine Bourriau
  pb 9780521032193

3 WAYS OF COMMUNICATING
  ed. D. H. Mellor
  pb 9780521019040

2 THE FRAGILE ENVIRONMENT
  ed. Laurie Friday and Ronald Laskey
  pb 9780521422666

1 ORIGINS
  ed. Andrew Fabian
  pb 9780521018197

SERENDIPITY

Fortune and the Prepared Mind

Edited by *Mark de Rond* and *Iain Morley*

CAMBRIDGE
UNIVERSITY PRESS

CAMBRIDGE UNIVERSITY PRESS

Cambridge, New York, Melbourne, Madrid, Cape Town, Singapore,
São Paulo, Delhi, Dubai, Tokyo, Mexico City

Cambridge University Press
The Edinburgh Building, Cambridge CB2 8RU, UK

Published in the United States of America by Cambridge University Press, New York

www.cambridge.org
Information on this title: www.cambridge.org/9780521181815

First published 2010

Printed in the United Kingdom at the University Press, Cambridge

A catalogue record for this publication is available from the British Library

Library of Congress Cataloguing in Publication data
Serendipity : fortune and the prepared mind / edited by Mark de Rond, Iain Morley.
    p.   cm. – (Darwin college lectures)
Includes index.
ISBN 978-0-521-18181-5 (pbk.)
1. Chance.   2. Serendipity.   3. Coincidence.   4. Synchronicity.   5. Fortune.
I. Rond, Mark de.   II. Morley, Iain, 1975–   III. Title.   IV. Series.
BD595.S47   2010
001.2 – dc22   2010020574

ISBN 978-0-521-18181-5 Paperback

Contents

List of figures   *page* viii
List of tables   x
Acknowledgements   xi

Introduction   Fortune and the prepared mind   1
IAIN MORLEY AND MARK DE ROND

1   The stratigraphy of serendipity   11
SUSAN E. ALCOCK

2   Understanding humans: serendipity and anthropology   27
RICHARD LEAKEY

3   HIV and the naked ape   45
ROBIN A. WEISS

4   Cosmological serendipity   65
SIMON SINGH

5   Serendipity in astronomy   73
ANDREW C. FABIAN

6   Serendipity in physics   91
RICHARD FRIEND

7   Liberalism and uncertainty   109
OLIVER LETWIN

8   The unanticipated pleasures of the writing life   123
SIMON WINCHESTER

Notes on the contributors   143
Index   147

Figures

Figure 1   A 'Richter scale' of human annual mortality.   *page* 63

Figure 2   NASA image of Io showing active volcanoes.   74

Figure 3   Serendipitous discoveries combine luck (or chance),
            preparedness and aim.   75

Figure 4   A schematic representation of some parts of
            Discovery Space.   76

Figure 5   The Crab Nebula.   79

Figure 6   Gamma-ray light curve of the soft gamma-ray
            repeater SGR1806.   80

Figure 7   A double Einstein ring caused by gravitational
            lensing.   83

Figure 8   Galaxies in a rich cluster.   84

Figure 9   Chandra X-ray image of the centre of the Perseus
            cluster of galaxies.   85

Figure 10   Velocity of the star 51 Peg along our line of sight.   85

Figure 11   Some Keck discoveries.   88

Figure 12   Foreground – weak green light emissions from an
            early polymer light-emitting diode enclosed in a
            vacuum chamber; background – laboratory
            whiteboard with artwork attributed to Karl Ziemelis
            (copyright University of Cambridge and Karl
            Ziemelis).   92

Figure 13   Top left: the Durham route to polyacetylene. Bottom
            left: FET structures formed with polyacetylene.
            Bottom right: transistor switching characteristics
            (copyright University of Cambridge).   94

Figure 14   Polymer light-emitting diode structure (copyright
            University of Cambridge).   95

Figures

Figure 15   Bound copies of the *Physical Review* in the Rayleigh
Library in the Cavendish Laboratory for 1960 and for
2005 (copyright R. H. Friend).   103
Figure 16   Early stage demonstration of a flexible electronic
paper display (copyright Plastic Logic Ltd).   106

Tables

Table 1 Origin of human viral infections   *page* 49
Table 2 Geographic origin of recently emerged human infections   55

Acknowledgements

The chapters in this book are derived from the talks given during the 23rd Darwin College Lecture Series, between January and March 2008. The editors are very grateful to the Master, Professor William Brown, the vice-Master, Professor Andy Fabian, and to the rest of Darwin College for hosting the series, and to Dr Jennifer Gates, for her work suggesting and inviting contributors to the series in the formative stages of its organization. We are also indebted to Professor Robin Weiss for producing his excellent talk at very short notice, and to Professor Ron Laskey for engaging Professor Weiss, to Professor Tony Cox and all who helped with the audio-visual facilities, to the members of college who performed essential ushering duties, and to Janet Gibson for all of her excellent correspondence with the speakers and essential facilitation of progress of the series and the book. Finally, we are grateful to the series editor, Richard Fisher, and to the Syndics of Cambridge University Press, for their continued support of this series.

Introduction
Fortune and the prepared mind

IAIN MORLEY AND MARK DE ROND

Serendipity was recently voted the most popular word in the English language. From only a handful of references in the late 1950s, a Google search today reveals nearly 8 million references (up from 3 million references a year ago). Ironically, 'serendipity' is also one of the most frequently queried words in the dictionary, and one of the hardest to translate. It is typically used as synonymous with luck, chance or coincidence. Thus, nearly one in ten of the most cited scientific papers mention serendipity as contributing to breakthrough innovations (Campanario 1996). Aside from bringing us such powerful agents as aspirin, the contraceptive pill, penicillin, laughing gas, vaccination, vitamin K, amphetamine, antihistamines, benzodiazepines, quinine, insulin, sulfa drugs, valproic acid, propafenone, magainins, nitrogen mustard, nitroglycerin, warfarin, the smallpox vaccine and cloretazine, it produced Scotchgard, Teflon, Velcro, Nylon, the Post-it Note, Kodak's Weekender camera, the technology behind the HP Inkjet printer (based on seeing a coffee percolator at work), electromagnetism, photography, dynamite, the phonograph, X-rays, radioactivity, and even Ivory Soap, liquorice allsorts and Coca Cola (patented, in 1886, as 'Pemberton's French Wine Coca' for medicinal purposes, as a nerve and tonic stimulant and a possible cure for headaches). In sum, the proposition that the process of discovery has a distinct logic may have been vastly overstated (Simontan 2004: 7). Yet, being what we are – fallible human beings with a penchant for predictability and control – we continue our vast investments into powerful statistical tools, automation, advances in molecular biology and novel technologies, so as to squeeze every last drop

Serendipity, edited by Mark de Rond and Iain Morley.
Published by Cambridge University Press. © Darwin College 2010.

of success out of scientific discovery programmes. In today's research, how much scope, if any, remains for serendipity? Looking behind, how justified are we to attribute past discoveries to serendipity? What is serendipity really?

The answers to such questions may lie in part in serendipity's history and etymological origins. Serendipity has a colourful history. As early as 1679, Robert Hooke alluded to the importance of serendipity in advancing research, describing invention as 'being but a lucky bitt of chance'. 'We shall quickly find', he wrote, 'that the number of considerable observations and Inventions this way collected will a hundred fold out-strip those that are found by Design.'[1] Joseph Priestley, writing in 1775, corroborated Hooke's conclusion by stating that 'more is owing to what we call chance, that is, philosophically speaking, to the observation of events arising from unknown causes, than to any proper design, or preconceived theory'.[2] Likewise, the physicist and Nobel laureate Percy Bridgman commented: 'how seldom the course of scientific development has been the logical course . . . Much more often the course of development is determined by factors which are quite adventitious as far as any connection goes with immediate human purpose', as did the French biologist Charles Richet: 'It will be a rather humiliating profession of faith, since I attribute a considerable role to chance.'[3] So too did Michel de Montaigne, attributing success in medicine principally to good fortune (Thiry-Cherques 2005). Claude Bernard wrote that ideas are often born by chance; Robert Root-Berstein (1989) thought invention to be guided by intention, but discovery by surprise; Martin Harwit, upon examining 43 cosmic phenomena concluded that about half took place in a 'serendipitous' manner (Campanario 1996). Particularly well-known examples include penicillin – or the discovery by Alexander Fleming of a mould with anti-bacterial properties in one of his cultures, a discovery which he made twice (1919 and 1928), and one which put him on the trail of similar observations by Tyndall, Roberts, Pasteur and Joubert, and Duchesne – and the elucidation of the DNA molecule by James Watson

---

[1] As quoted in Merton and Barber 2004, p. 161
[2] ibid. p. 162
[3] ibid. pp. 164–5

and Francis Crick in 1953. We wish colleagues 'good luck', not to insinuate that they are incapable but because we all realize that effort alone is hardly sufficient in making breakthrough discoveries (Rescher 1995). Our lack of omniscience, if nothing else, leaves plenty scope for luck.

What is curious is that using serendipity as synonymous with luck seems far removed from its etymology. Horace Walpole, in 1754, wrote of a critical discovery he had made, of an exciting old Arabic tale. One fine day, so goes the tale, three princes from Serendip (Ceylon, or modern-day Sri Lanka) were sent by their father on a prolonged journey to acquire empirical experience as part of their training. Misfortune befell the princes when happening upon a camel driver, who enquired of them about a camel he had lost. Though the princes had not seen the animal, they were nonetheless able to accurately describe it: it was blind in one eye, lacking a tooth, and lame. Furthermore, the camel was carrying butter on one side and honey on the other, and was being ridden by a pregnant woman. Their description was so accurate, in fact, that the camel owner accused the princes of having stolen his camel, and formally charged them in the emperor's court. However, in the presence of Emperor Behram, it became clear that the princes were entirely innocent, having merely pieced together various events. They explained that they thought the camel blind in the right eye because the grass had been cropped only on the left side of the road. They inferred that it was missing a tooth from the bits of chewed grass scattered across the road. Its footprints seemed to suggest that the animal was lame and dragging one foot. Also, finding ants on one side of the road and flies on the other, they concluded that the camel must have been carrying butter on the ants' side, and honey on the other. Finally, as for the presence of a pregnant woman, a combination of carnal desires on the part of the princes, and imprints of hands on the ground sufficed to bring about this final conclusion.

Clearly, the princes did far more than make chance observations. The tale is instructive precisely because the princes relied on their ability to recombine observations and deduce 'correct' – or meaningful – associations so as to generate a surprisingly effective (and, as it happens, entirely accurate) plot. To redefine serendipity as a consequence of recombining observations into unusual but meaningful associations suggests it is a close relative of creativity. To use an analogy, serendipity reflects the ability to create a tune from a handful of musical scores from different genres and composers, torn into small bits by an enterprising toddler, and scattered randomly across the floor. Serendipity results not from reconstructing existing harmonies but from recombining small sequences of musical notes into something unusual, something altogether different. The ability to *imagine* such unusual but meaningful combinations lies at the heart of those drug discoveries credited almost exclusively to luck. After all, many a man floated in water before Archimedes, and apples fell from trees as long ago as the Garden of Eden.[4]

The ambiguity surrounding 'serendipity', in terms of etymology and practice, is reflected in eight beautifully crafted chapters. Their contributors are all masters of their respective arts, whose personal and professional experiences have given them unique perspectives on the diversity of forms and roles that serendipity can take.

Sue Alcock sets the concept of serendipity in the context of the human past, exploring the origin and subsequent 'coming of age' of the term itself – both of which are recent in the extreme when considered in light of our history. But is it really a recent concept? She goes on to explore, from the perspective of archaeology and classics (and classical archaeology in particular), the *stratigraphy* of the concept – the layers of its history and its meanings. The role of serendipity in archaeology, and in her own experiences as a practising archaeologist, forms the latter part of the chapter. Here we see the extent to which serendipity can be either embraced or denied in research, and all the combinations of planning, expertise and fortuitous circumstances that progress our exploration and understanding of the past.

The combination of preparedness and readiness to seize unexpected opportunity is a strong theme in Richard Leakey's contribution, as he touches upon the role of serendipity in his own, and in his parents', remarkable careers. But he goes on to focus also on the extent to which this concept can, or cannot, be applied to the discovered as well as the discoverer – the process of evolution, and human evolution in particular – and its role in the formation of the fossil record from which we draw our conclusions. He concludes by considering the extent to

---

[4] Walter Cannon, as quoted in Merton and Barber 2004, pp. 171–2

which we, as a species, will need to rely on our ability to sagaciously exploit our changing circumstances, and our adaptations, in the coming years, as changes in climate transform the world in which we have developed.

The relationships between humans and the natural world also form the core of Robin Weiss's contribution. The story of Alexander Fleming's discovery of penicillin is often cited as an example of serendipitous discovery, but the relationship between disease and exploitation of chance (albeit often lacking in sagacity) goes much further than this. Robin Weiss's work on infectious diseases, and in particular the HIV virus, provides a very particular perspective on the role of opportunism in human biology generally, and on microbiology specifically. Humans have in many cases constituted accidental hosts for infectious agents which, whilst not having 'prepared minds', have proven collectively highly adaptable to their new environment. But mutations in humans have also fortuitously led to resistance to some of these, and consequently been selected for too. He discusses how changes in microbes and parasites have taken advantage of human biology, and the evolution of human biology, and how our tracing of those changes can also tell us about the prehistory of our own species.

Simon Singh has written extensively on the topic of serendipity in science, and here gives an inspiring overview of the combination of chance events and the sagacity of certain individuals in the discovery of some of the most fundamental evidence for the nature and formation of the Universe. This includes the very origins of radio astronomy, as well as the detection of solar radio waves and the 'echo' from the Big Bang at the very beginning of the Universe (and taking in Velcro, Post-it notes and Viagra along the way). What these cases all have in common is the readiness of the researchers concerned to embrace the opportunity presented, often in the face of extreme frustration at the unexpected event.

Drawing upon his own work in the field of astronomy, Andy Fabian returns to the very concept of serendipity itself, and how the factors constituting serendipitous discoveries interact. He explores the relationship between preparedness, luck and aim in serendipitous discovery – and, in fact, the importance of the involvement of all three of those axes in truly novel discoveries. In discussing some of the most important discoveries in the field of astronomy, and the very way in which the field progresses, he highlights the fact that the relationship between preparedness, aim and luck is not acknowledged as fully as it might advantageously be in the funding of research.

This critique forms a key element too of Richard Friend's essay, drawing upon his own and other critical discoveries in the realm of materials science and physics. He outlines a sequence of highly important discoveries (in the field of superconductivity in particular) which were made possible as a consequence of the right observations being made at the right time – when the necessary equipment was available – often in ways that could not have been anticipated. Not being constrained by 'received wisdom' or even 'understood laws' of physics is critical, and planning and method must be coupled with acting upon observation of unexpected phenomena. He presents a set of rules for the enthusiastic researcher who wishes to genuinely make new discoveries and progress in their field – not least of which is the importance of not being constrained by the structures of modern academic funding and refereeing, which in many respects fundamentally restrict such progress. He ends on the promising note that the prospects for serendipitous discovery, and its value, are as great now as they have ever been.

The role and management of unexpected events forms the basis of Oliver Letwin's contribution, which explores the very nature of liberal politics. Different (liberal or autocratic) modes of government revolve around the balance between government action and citizen reaction, and the effect of unanticipated outcomes on the effectiveness of policies with expected consequences. He argues that government action will typically only be effective through the *mediation* of uncertain citizen reaction, rather than the attempt to extinguish uncertainty. That mediation involves the exercise of judgement about the uncertain reaction and, perhaps, the ability to take advantage of unanticipated circumstances.

He argues that accepting the concept of uncertainty of reaction should change the way that politicians operate – a timely observation given the uncertain times most of us experience today in Britain as well as abroad. A liberal politician must create frameworks in which the reactions and decision-making of the population take place, the frameworks minimizing the unpredictability of those reactions, without being prescriptive. He goes on to discuss the changing nature of these relationships between uncertainty and information in the modern world, and how this should affect the nature of political activity.

Being a professional writer would appear to require some particular traits – not least independence, spontaneity and a diligently creative approach to recognizing and developing subject matter from the world around. But Simon Winchester's engaging personal account of serendipitous events in his own career also highlights the core theme of the other chapters of this book – namely, the importance of an underlying ability to recognize opportunities when you see them, and, most importantly, to act upon them.

It still remains to offer some explanation of the recent burgeoning in popularity of the concept of serendipity. Perhaps part of this is due to what might be called a 'lottery mentality': the appeal of the tacit suggestion that 'great things' can be discovered or achieved by anyone, if in the right place at the right time. As will be seen from the following chapters, merely being in the right place at the right time on its own is not, in fact, enough to lead to truly serendipitous discovery. Perhaps there is an inherent appeal to the sense that no matter how much planning or preparation is carried out, true discovery relies on some mercurial extra ingredient. Whilst this might be the case, the chapters that follow illustrate that dispensing with preparation and planning will certainly not facilitate the course of serendipity.

But perhaps a less cynical explanation might be offered. There seems to be an inclination (certainly in the popular reporting of discoveries in science and the human past) to seek to identify 'magic moments': *the* moment or *the* event that furthered our understanding of the natural world, of social interactions, even of humanity itself. Thus, for example, we speak of *the* missing link between higher primates and humans, *the* moment when humans began to walk upright, or started to paint representations of the world around them, *the* turning point in history which led to the First World War – the list goes on. Of course, in reality these are very rarely single moments, but concatenations of circumstances and potentials – the potentials to respond to those circumstances – and these concatenations are actually rarely unique and even more rarely retrospectively identified.

The idea of serendipity, and considerations of serendipitous occurrences, however, appeals very strongly to this inclination to identify 'magic moments' when significant turning points occurred. And they are particularly appealing in this respect because they *do*, in fact, combine both of the above scenarios: serendipitous events or discoveries very often *are* attributable to a single 'moment', but at the same time are entirely dependent upon the relationship between the right circumstances and the potential to respond to them in an advantageous way; the meeting of fortune and the preparation to identify and react to that fortune.

Often it is observations of tiny things that lead to conclusions regarding some of the greatest. But it is not in the observation itself that serendipity plays its role – that may only be *chance* – but it is in the responses to those observations, the attitude and expertise, *sagacity* of the observer, that births *serendipity* from chance.

A note on the cover image

The cover image shows the 3.6 million-year-old trail of footprints at Laetoli, Tanzania. The footprints were initially discovered by Andrew Hill, a member of Mary Leakey's archaeological team, in 1976, and were subsequently excavated by Leakey's team during 1978 and 1979. Hill spotted the first prints whilst ducking to avoid elephant dung thrown by a colleague (Tattersall 1995). Fortunately the expertise of the discoverers allowed the importance of the prints to be recognized and, as in the story of the Princes of Serendip, conclusions could be drawn about the individuals who created the trail.

The prints were created by three Australopithecine human ancestors, two adults and one juvenile, as they walked together across a newly fallen layer of volcanic ash, which hardened and set like concrete after a rain shower shortly afterwards (Stringer and Andrews 2005). One of the adults walked behind the other two individuals, stepping into the footprints created by the adult in front. The prints unequivocally illustrate that these human ancestors walked bipedally 3.6 million years ago.

The photograph was taken by Martha Demas in 1995, during a programme of preservation undertaken by the Getty Conservation Institute in collaboration with the Tanzanian Department of Antiquities (see

Agnew and Demas 1998). The editors are very grateful to Dr Demas, the Getty Conservation Institute and Donatius Kamamba at the Tanzanian Department of Antiquities for permission to reproduce this image.

References

Agnew, N. and M. Demas (1998) 'Preserving the Laetoli footprints', *Scientific American* 279(3), 44–5.

Campanario, J. M. (1996) 'Using citation classics to study the incidence of serendipity in scientific discovery', *Scientometrics* 37, 3–24.

Merton, R. and E. Barber (2004) *The Travels and Adventures of Serendipity.* Princeton, NJ: Princeton University Press.

Resher, N. (1995) *Luck: The Brilliant Randomness of Everyday Life.* Pittsburg, PA: Pittsburg University Press.

Root-Bernstein, R. S. (1989) *Discovering: Inventing and Solving Problems at the Frontiers of Scientific Knowledge.* Cambridge, MA: Harvard University Press.

Simonton, D. K. (2004) *Creativity in Science.* Cambridge: Cambridge University Press.

Stringer, C. and P. Andrews (2005) *The Complete World of Human Evolution.* London: Thames and Hudson.

Tattersall, I. (1995) *The Fossil Trail: How We Know What We Think We Know About Human Evolution.* Oxford: Oxford University Press.

Thiry-Cherques, H. R. (2004) 'Chance and fortune', *Organisation* 12(4), 590–600.

1   The stratigraphy of serendipity

SUSAN E. ALCOCK

Serendipity is a baby. A baby! The time depth, the stratigraphy, of the
word is, to a classicist, to an archaeologist, shallow in the extreme, its
inception hardly a blink away in time. But if the stratigraphy is shallow, it is also clear. Serendipity was born, on the written page at least,
28 January 1754, coined by Horace Walpole in a letter addressed to a
friend in Italy. What followed was a century or so of near neglect, then
a period of slow adoption and diffusion, before the explosion into today's
veritable carnival of usage. Serendipity is, as widely acknowledged, wildly
fashionable today – ranking, in recent online polls of 'most popular' words,
well above reliable standbys such as *Jesus*, or *money*. Numbers underline
the point, with recorded references in LexisNexis (a professional information service) zooming from a total of 2 in the 1960s to over 13,000 in
the 1990s (Merton 2004: 287), on Google from 600,000 in 2001 to over
11 million in 2008, and climbing. Such figures are not, admittedly, statis-
tically valid in any sense; nevertheless, they mark serendipity's meteoric
rise, its present rich level of exploitation.

What we appear to have, then, is a quite pleasingly demonstrated
pattern of invention, gradual transmission and wide-scale adoption. But
that is the last easy thing to be said about serendipity, a word that its own
inventor left somewhat confused in definition, and that has subsequently
undergone various transformations and, some would say, trivializations.
The intention in this essay is to play with this new baby of a word, with
the help and the perspectives of two disciplines deeply engaged with the
past – Classics and Archaeology (and principally my own field of Classical
Archaeology). This play will revolve around the notion of *stratigraphy*,

Serendipity, edited by Mark de Rond and Iain Morley.
Published by Cambridge University Press. © Darwin College 2010.

taken here as the study of temporal layering, of chronological depth, of the study of change over time. The questions are, beyond what we've already said of its short happy life: what can stratigraphic analysis do to, and do for, this Darwin Lecture subject? Is there a stratigraphy of serendipity?

Classics and Archaeology, my two chosen babysitters, will come at these questions from two quite different directions. For Classics, the stratigraphic dimension is more straightforward; the Greeks and Romans, after all, pre-dated Horace Walpole by a considerable degree. But might there nonetheless be a prehistory to the, as yet uncoined, term? To put it another way, did serendipity exist before its formal eighteenth-century christening? For Archaeology, the examination will instead revolve around the manner in which serendipitous discovery has aided the discipline's basic mission of identifying and interpreting change over time (a circumstance, incidentally, that not all archaeologists acknowledge). Both discussions will springboard us, in conclusion, into thinking about possible strata yet to come, about the possible futures of serendipity.

Before proceeding, however, some definitions and clarifications are required, for serendipity comes in different flavours. At one end of the spectrum, as a kind of lowest common denominator, the word has come to mean chance, coincidence, sheer dumb luck. For example, at its most sweetly banal, take this posting from an online dating service, now 'immortalized' on *Wiktionary*: 'The most random serendipity brought the two of us together, and now, we are happily married! If I was just 15 seconds slower, I'd have never met her!' This is the more relaxed, some have said 'vague', version of serendipity (let us call it 'serendipity lite'), and it has launched a thousand dubious hair salons and day spas, tacky gift shops and more (Boyle, 'Serendipity', n.d.).

Horace Walpole himself, on 28 January 1754, seems to have had something more nuanced, something stricter and stronger, in mind. This emerges in Walpole's letter to Horace Mann, discussing an observation just made about a recently acquired painting.

> This discovery indeed is almost of that kind which I call *serendipity*, a very expressive word, which as I have nothing better to tell you, I shall endeavour to explain to you: you will understand it better by the

derivation than by the definition. I once read a silly fairy tale, called *The Three Princes of Serendip*: as their highnesses travelled, they were always making discoveries, by accidents and sagacity, of things which they were not in quest of: for instance, one of them discovered that a mule blind of the right eye had travelled the same road lately, because the grass was eaten only on the left side, where it was worse than on the right – now do you understand *serendipity?* One of the most remarkable instances of this *accidental sagacity* (for you must observe that *no* discovery of a thing you *are* looking for comes under this description) was of my Lord Shaftsbury, who happening to dine at Lord Chancellor Clarendon's, found out the marriage of the Duke of York and Mrs. Hyde, by the respect with which her mother treated her at table.

(quoted in Remer 1965: 6; emphasis in original)

Thus the launching of serendipity, a much-parsed passage. For many have remarked how Walpole here provides peculiarly obscure examples (from hungry mules to the noble Duke of York): examples that from the very beginning leave the word ambiguous. Just some of the questions left hanging: does the thing found have to be important, or result in significant consequences? Does the thing found have to be a 'good thing'? Might the thing found have been expected to be found? How much is due to luck and how much to the skill of the person looking? 'Now do you understand *serendipity?*', Walpole asks – and the answer ever since has been a slightly puzzled: 'sort of'.

For all that, there remains some consensus here for a stricter definition: 'serendipity strong' revolves around the finding of what you didn't know you were looking for; and it involves both accidents and sagacity. The latter is an important dimension to stress, given the emphasis of 'serendipity lite' on chance, luck, happenstance; sagacity has too often been lost in the shuffle of subsequent usage. The rest of this essay will engage with 'serendipity strong', and 'serendipity lite', though it will hunt particularly along the lines of the former. For the full story of serendipity's wonderful, twisty evolution, one can turn to a wonderful, twisty book, Robert Merton and Elinor Barber's *The Travels and Adventures of Serendipity*, written in the 1950s but put aside unpublished, appearing (unchanged) only in 2004 (Merton and Barber 2004). It is by no means serendipitous, I suspect, to find this concept chosen for a Darwin Lecture series a mere four years later.

So is there a hidden time depth to serendipity, a pre-Walpolean existence to the concept? This can, and should, be asked of multiple periods
and cultures (a volume generally exploring the 'prehistory' of serendipity
would make a wonderful companion piece to Merton and Barber). Here we
can only quickly explore the situation vis-à-vis the Greeks and Romans.
Whatever the precise derivation from Walpole's 'silly fairy tale, called *The
Three Princes of Serendip*', 'serendipity' certainly isn't from the Greek, nor
the Latin. But did the ancient classical civilizations of the Mediterranean
possess and enjoy the concept anyway?

To be honest, the answer expected was yes, of course: if largely based
on the classicist's errant assumption that the Greeks did everything first.
Instead, my conclusion seems to be a rather unsatisfying 'sort of'. What
we find in antiquity is closer to 'serendipity lite': to findings of chance,
matters of luck. Both the Greeks and Romans had a pervasive, highly
developed concept of fortune, both represented by female personifica-
tions (Tyche to the Greeks, Fortuna to the Romans). The interventions
of these forces in human lives were recognized as frequent, for good or
ill. More specifically, the Greeks had a term *hermaion*, for an unexpected
piece of good luck, a godsend, a windfall – something not looked for, but
given out of the blue. Such things were perceived as the gift of Hermes
(hence *hermaion*): Hermes, the god of boundaries and of boundary crossing, the god of invention, of wit – the trickster god. If any deity is to
oversee the slippery concept of serendipity, Hermes seems just about
perfect.

In aid of this paper, I quizzed many classicists for examples of serendipitous behaviour, and was presented with a head-scratching range of 'how
about this?': battles unexpectedly won, comets or eclipses perfectly timed
to serve as omens, vital military dispatches lost, and more. All acceptable
instances, as far as they go. But examples of the stricter, stronger version
of serendipity – the finding of what you didn't know you were looking for, through both accidents and sagacity – those have proven more
elusive.

The big apparent exception to this pattern, the original Eureka!
moment, comes of course with Archimedes in his bath. Thanks to his
position at the court of the king of Syracuse, Archimedes, the renowned
third-century BC mathematician and inventor, was charged with

detecting a potential fraud, the debasement of a golden votive crown. To quote our first account of the event:

> Charged with this commission, he by chance went to a bath, and being in the vessel, perceived that, as his body became immersed, the water ran out of the vessel. Whence, catching at the method to be adopted for the solution of the proposition, he immediately followed it up, leapt out of the vessel in joy, and, returning home naked, cried out with a loud voice that he had found that of which he was in search, for he continued exclaiming, in Greek, εὕρηκα, (I have found it out).
>
> (Vitruvius, *De architectura* 9.9–10)

Now that is a great ta-da! moment. And, like many such triumphant scenes, it has been queried and nibbled at ever since. The science has been questioned; the event's historicity has been questioned; the first teller of the story is the much later (first-century BC) Roman architect Vitruvius (whose account emerged in the course of a discussion about how architects deserve more honour than wrestlers). And, finally, one could argue that, in the absolute strictest sense, this isn't 'strong' serendipity – unless Archimedes was looking for something else in the bath (soap, his rubber ducky) and discovered hydrostatics. But it remains the best ancient example we possess.

And that appears to be the pattern from Classics so far. 'Serendipity lite', yes, the workings of chance and fortune, everywhere: but signs of the stronger brew of accidents and sagacity are far less visible. This may, of course, simply reflect the massive rate of loss of ancient texts; very little of Archimedes' own output, for example, has made it through the ages. Others might cut more directly to the chase, and suggest that ancient science was not sufficiently devoted to rigorous experimentation. A failure to emphasize empirical research thus meant a failure to generate those unpredictable, Eureka! moments on which serendipity feeds. One influential voice against such a view would be that of Geoffrey Lloyd (erstwhile Master of Darwin College), who instead defends the ancient 'ambitions of curiosity' (Lloyd 2002; Lloyd 1973: 177–8). Lloyd has, however, pointed to other possible factors militating against the serendipitous. A relative lack of institutional support for the sciences, coupled with a need to 'make reputation' through disputation and competition: these are not conditions to encourage the recognition, admission and celebration of accidents, of mistakes. Serendipity might strike, in other words, but rhetorical skills could equally be employed to cover its tracks (a pattern seen again later in this essay).

Perhaps even more fundamentally, Lloyd emphasizes the conditions in which ancient researchers worked: usually in isolation, usually lacking close interlocutors to push and notice and develop (Lloyd 2002: e.g. 146–7). Archimedes, for example, lamented the loss of a friend and mathematical colleague, not least because no one else seemed capable or interested in picking up where that individual had left off. Rather plaintively, Archimedes wrote: 'though many years have elapsed since Conon's death, I do not find that any one of the problems has been stirred by a single person' (*On Spirals*, preface; Lloyd 2002: 135). In a world of isolated scholars, often in competition, lacking a community of inquiry, of mutual exchange: in such a milieu new ideas and research trajectories could be generated, only to perish unnoticed.

At this point, we can introduce another dimension to this conceit of stratigraphy, and that is the time lag that serendipity often requires to reach fruition. By no means is the first observer of a phenomenon always the one who actually experiences the Eureka! moment; serendipity might take time to strike. But in the world of ancient science, with no readily sustainable genealogy of ideas, no open reporting of mistakes, no immediate cohort to be curious: in such an environment we can imagine the baby serendipity being strangled in its cradle.

This has, of course, been a very cursory exploration of the intersection of Classics and serendipity, but two conclusions would seem to emerge. First, that any final classical answer to Walpole's question – 'now do you understand *serendipity?*' – is far from transparent. And second, that there appear to be reasons why the ancients didn't have a word for it.

In some ways, Archaeology and serendipity are somewhat more natural, comfortable playmates than the austere Classics, not least in that they are more roughly contemporary, with the early, 'speculative', stages of archaeological development not that far from Walpole's eighteenth-century world (Piggott 1989). Indeed, preeminent early adopters of the term included 'the world of "discoverers" of all kinds', with Merton and Barber specifically naming antiquarians, book collectors and scientists: all near neighbours of the early practitioners of archaeology (2004: 9).

What I prefer to address, however, are more recent passages in the intersection of serendipity and archaeology, which is far from the happiest of relationships. Imagine yourself on a bus, dropping into conversation with an elderly gentleman who asks you what you do. You tell him that you are an archaeologist. To which he replies: 'That must be wonderful, for the only thing you have to be to succeed is lucky' (an encounter reported by Lewis Binford, an influential figure in the scientifically oriented, so-called 'New Archaeology' of the later twentieth century; Binford 1983: 19). Such awkward conversations have been experienced and handled with varying degrees of grace, by innumerable practitioners of the field. We know what people are thinking ... of apparently random, fortunate finds, lucky strikes: Howard Carter peering in to see 'wonderful things' in King Tut-Ankh-Amun's tomb; Ötzi the Iceman, temporarily revealed in his bed of ice; the terracotta army of the First Emperor – found by a team of well diggers. Surely each an *hermaion*; surely archaeologists are the beloved of serendipity? Amusing to the outsider, the assumption nonetheless irks, and thus archaeologists tend to spurn this embrace. Consult the index of any of the major archaeological textbooks on the market and turn to 'S'. You will jump from sequence dating to Serpent Mound, sediments to settlements, semiotics to Shaft Graves, Sennacherib to Seti I. Serendipity is nowhere to be seen.

There is wrong on both sides here. First, archaeology is more than a matter of happy fortune; considering archaeologists no more than the hapless children of Providence is obviously a careless application of 'serendipity lite' in action. On the other hand, archaeology's rejection of serendipity is disingenuous, for the discipline is profoundly, and not irresponsibly, a serendipitous practice. As we explore, as we investigate, as we look for what we are looking for – inexorably, inevitably, we encounter and must deal with the unexpected. Sometimes this can be most unwelcome, as when discoveries are made (requiring substantial investment in documentation, conservation, publication) that lie far outside the original research questions and interests of an investigator or project. In such cases, serendipity can indeed be a jokester, and a pain. But it can also be transformative, drawing archaeologists into what Robert Merton, in his 1957 book *Social Theory and Social Structure*, referred to as the 'serendipity pattern': the experience of 'observing an unanticipated, anomalous and strategic datum which becomes the occasion for developing a new theory or for extending an existing theory' (1957: 276; Maniscalco 1998).

Two sketches of this 'serendipity pattern' in action can be presented. Both delivered a swift kick to, and made a lasting impression upon, the field of archaeology. We can begin with the very measurement of time itself, and the power of radiocarbon dating. Radiocarbon, or Carbon-14, dating can offer absolute dates (within certain parameters) by measuring the rate of decay of Carbon-14 in appropriate archaeological samples. As pioneered by Willard Libby in the mid twentieth century, for the first time the global construction of completely independent, absolute chronologies appeared feasible: chronologies that could be matched and partnered with evidence from other sources, such as Egyptian historical records or dendrochronology (the science of tree ring dating). This, the first radiocarbon revolution, wowed the archaeological world, and Willard Libby won the 1960 Nobel Prize for Chemistry.

If the discovery seemed almost too good to be true, it was. It rapidly became clear that initial radiocarbon results were off-kilter, disagreeably disagreeing on dates reliably pinned down in other ways. Dates were coming in as too early, a fact for which variations in cosmic radiation were promptly blamed. Nothing daunted, methods to 'adjust' radiocarbon findings were evolved, with calibrations depending on an extensive tree ring sequence. The resulting 'second radiocarbon revolution' is where the notion of looking for one thing, only to find another, enters the fray. For as this 'tweaking' of curves and dates worked very nicely in sorting out chronologies for the eastern Mediterranean and Egypt, it simultaneously blew apart previous theories of connections between the Mediterranean and prehistoric Europe. This revolution rendered unfeasible theories of cultural diffusion in which all good flowed from the East (*ex oriente lux*), and destroyed conceptions of a world where it was thought the Mycenaeans, the Greeks (who else?), had built Stonehenge. The second radiocarbon revolution, by imposing a chronological 'fault line', a caesura, between these two zones, essentially forced an entirely new, and still evolving, conception of European prehistory (Renfrew 1979).

My second example is more personal, since it involves the kind of archaeology I chiefly practise. Regional survey, as this mode of

reconnaissance is called, involves teams walking the countryside seeking traces of past human activity, recovering – from a surface palimpsest
of ruined structures, discarded potsherds and figurines, broken roof tiles,
remains of graves, and more – data that reveal modes of life within, and
uses of, the rural landscape across the *longue durée*. Regional survey takes
place in all corners of the world, but the classical lands (the Mediterranean,
and particularly Greece) today rank as among the most intensively scru-
tinized portions of the globe (Snodgrass 1987; Barker and Mattingly
1999–2000).

Survey is by nature a most serendipitous beast. You walk and look –
but in a surface palimpsest stretching from the Palaeolithic to the present,
there is no easy way to predict what you might find, and in what patterns. Nor, however specific one's period interest or problem orientation,
can you ethically disregard the temporal smorgasbord that lies before
you, silently demanding attention and interpretation. This leads not only
to much collaborative work on regional survey teams, but to strange,
serendipitous forms of knowledge acquisition: classically trained archaeologists comfortable with Neolithic pottery; Bronze Age prehistorians
who can date Turkish pipe stems or work in Ottoman archives. Indeed,
the now improving study of sadly neglected periods in Greece's past, such
as Roman or mediaeval and post-mediaeval times, has been much driven
by the promptings of survey discovery (Alcock 1993; Lock and Sanders
1996). This is just one arena for Merton's 'serendipity pattern', where
unanticipated, even perhaps originally unwelcome, observations trigger
the amplification and extension of existing thinking.

To push this further, one could argue that survey archaeology in the
Mediterranean was 'out of the box' from its very beginnings. Classical
archaeology, as has been widely recognized, for much of its disciplinary
history focused on the urban, the urbane, the monumental, the pretty,
the valuable. Survey archaeology, with its embrace of rural grubbiness,
quotidian life, and decidedly fragmentary, unappealing surface finds, was
a radical, and initially resisted, mode of analysis. So where did it come
from?

In answering that question, the workings of strong serendipity must
undoubtedly take a bow. The grandfather project of Greek survey, what
ultimately became known as the University of Minnesota Messenia

Expedition (UMME), began its work, in the 1950s in the southwest of mainland Greece, with a very limited mission. The goal was to map out the administrative structure of a Late Bronze Age, a Mycenaean, kingdom. This ambition was spurred by the (then) recent discovery and translation of Linear B tablets, texts written in an early form of Greek which outlined the territorial holdings and organization of the so-called 'Palace of Nestor' at Pylos. UMME's original plan was simply to locate, on the ground, the various toponyms identified on the tablets – and that was all. But as the archaeological team travelled from place to place in this Greek countryside, they found more than they were looking for. They walked into, fell over, numerous other traces of all periods of the past: Middle Bronze Age tombs, classical acropoleis, mediaeval roadways – all previously unknown, all unexpected, but not to be ignored (McDonald and Rapp 1972). From that basic recognition there developed a more inclusive exploration of local history, and a highly influential model for regional work in the classical lands. In other words, understandings of the archaeological landscapes of the Mediterranean world owe much to the workings of serendipity.

One additional spin was previously added to the conceit of stratigraphy – the notion of 'time lag', in which serendipity bides its time to strike. In the world of ancient science, it was suggested that this process could well be truncated, that ideas could perish in limbo. Such delayed gratification, by contrast, is increasingly familiar in present day archaeological practice. One compelling example comes from, oddly enough, the deployment of spy satellite imagery. While making the world safe for democracy, these orbital eyes were not at all seeking to document archaeological sites, nor yet landscape change – but that is what they did. With formal declassification beginning in the 1990s, archaeologists have since feasted on this serendipitously available, extremely welcome, information (Fowler 2004).

That is an example in many ways from out of the blue, but archaeological research itself can generate material for the long-term operation of serendipity. One example that I have explored is the practice of ancestor – or hero – cult, conducted in later, historic periods at prehistoric tombs, such as the famous tholos (beehive) tombs of Greece. Early archaeologists (including Heinrich Schliemann, excavator of Mycenae and Troy) dug such monuments with their eye firmly fixed on the question of who built them, and who was buried in them (not least celebrities such as Atreus, Agamemnon, Clytemnestra, Minyas). The discovery in such tombs, in passing, of later pottery or votives, later signs of religious sacrifice or feasting, was essentially disregarded, being considered garbage or intrusive junk when it was mentioned at all.

The stakes could get higher still, as when Schliemann and his compatriots excavated impressive looking mounds in the plains of windy Troy, hunting eagerly for the tombs of Achilles, of Patroklos, or of Hector. Their hopes were embarrassingly dashed, when these mounds were revealed instead as prehistoric settlements (the Tomb of Achilles) or natural hillocks (the Tomb of Patroklos), artificially enhanced, 'faked up', in later antiquity to look imposing. Worse yet, the biggest, the most outstanding of all tumuli in the plain did prove to be a tomb, but not that of a Homeric hero. Instead it was dated securely to the Roman period, apparently erected to one Festus, a favourite of the Roman emperor Caracalla (in an act of 'mad extravagance' by a 'vain fool', as Schliemann raged). For all the visible mortification, it is to the credit of the red-faced excavators that these discomfiting discoveries were at least documented, if hastily set aside.

Yet these in-their-time depressing datum points, for so long lying fallow, are today being reactivated, offering insights into the commemorative landscapes of all periods at Troy, insights into the memorial practices and uses of 'the past in the past'. Without launching into interpretive detail, the point here is that as the theoretical and conceptual environment of a discipline alters, old and dormant data are rendered newly applicable, newly desirable. Later 'junk' in old tombs? There is a story there to be told (Alcock 2004). In a field that generates as many random finds as archaeology does, such re-energizing rediscovery can and should happen all the time. Yet what this possibility calls for, of course, is good record keeping, ample documentation, detailed publication and unbiased preservation of as much evidence as possible. These are tall orders, not least financially and logistically, but the stratigraphy of serendipity demands them.

Surprisingly, it would be difficult to identify many additional, obvious case studies of the interplay of archaeology and serendipity. Not,

I would argue, because the serendipity pattern is rare, but because archaeologists – as other scholars – tend to fight it, and to hide it. More lies behind this reaction than mere resentment about being thought 'just lucky'. Rather it involves the very construction of the discipline itself. Reputations have had to be built (and spared); publications have had to be authoritative, linear and rational; archaeological 'whoopsies' (however sagaciously handled) have had to be muted, or erased. The attraction of retrospective prophecy ('I saw it coming all along!') consciously or unconsciously enters into play (Merton and Barber 2004: 19–20). The possible existence of these same protective filters at work in the ancient world has already been noted. Moreover, all these phenomena are, of course, familiar from other modern scholarly domains, not least the world of the 'hard sciences': though there a far more healthy, public debate reigns about the place and value of serendipity. On the one hand, the phenomenon's sheer flukiness would seem to make a mockery of research design and control, while on the other, it is hard to argue with the value of an outcome like penicillin (see Merton and Barber 2004 for an exploration of parallels, or divergences, between different disciplines and their reaction to serendipity).

To conclude. What about possible strata yet to come? What about the possible futures of serendipity? In archaeology, the outlook would in some ways seem bright. In very recent decades a new theoretical and conceptual atmosphere has infused the discipline, moving away from the more rigorously 'scientific' research agenda of the later twentieth century (the 'New Archaeology' of Lewis Binford and others). This new mood (which travels under the now somewhat baggy label of 'post-processualism') encourages the exploration of individual, unpredictable experience in the past, while at the same time admitting the vicissitudes and vagaries of archaeological practice in the present (Hodder and Hutson 2003). Moreover, new technologies of media recording – the ubiquity of digital cameras, the ease of video streaming, the accessibility of blogs – all make the creation of multiple, alternative, and sometimes subversive, documentary records in the field entirely possible, and indeed advantageous. Accidents, apparent mistakes, will become harder and harder to hide. This should, by rights, encourage the 'second strike' of sagacity, and the serendipitous recognition of new possibilities.

That is the optimistic prediction. On the other hand, it is clear that technologies and circumstances are equally conspiring to restrain serendipity's antic quality as well. Scientific forms of remote sensing such as aerial imagery or geophysical testing allow us increasingly to 'see below the surface', to see, at least partially, just what we are getting into, before we get into it. Now making the practice of archaeology less 'chancy' need not be a bad thing; such pre-screening definitely saves time, labour and money, items inevitably in short supply. Moreover, as the threat to global cultural heritage ramps up alarmingly, and as more and more archaeological landscapes are being destroyed through the ravages of everything from urban sprawl to global warming, anything that aids archaeological efficiency is to be applauded. But what do we abandon, if we give up serendipity?

This is, of course, part of a much larger and significant debate. For the rumbles are coming in, from various directions, warning that serendipity (in the strong sense) is under threat. Technological innovations again play an important role here, with the internet directively providing instant answers; with electronic journals hyperlinking you straight from what you are reading to what they think you should read next. As budgets tighten, research expectations narrow and training specializes, the relaxed ability sagaciously to recognize happy accidents, and the time and support to chase them, seems imperilled. Efficiency, yes, utility, yes: but as scholarly pathways clarify and solidify, it is harder to bound off in new directions – to further this particular baby's travels and adventures.

If considering the stratigraphy of serendipity does nothing else, it can remind us of two things. First, in its strongest sense, serendipity can be a powerful transformative force, generating the best possible kinds of shock and awe – if in its own sweet time. And second, we must remember that the existence of serendipity is not automatic, it is not an absolute given. Serendipity need not have a future. And that would be a loss indeed.

References

Alcock, S. E. (1993) *Graecia Capta: The Landscapes of Roman Greece.* Cambridge: Cambridge University Press.

Alcock, S. E. (2004) 'Material witness: an archaeological context for the Heroikos', in E. B. Aitken and J. K. B. MacLean, *Philostratus's Heroikos: Religion and Cultural Identity in the Third Century C.E.* Atlanta: Society of Biblical Literature.

Barker, G. and D. Mattingly, eds. (1999–2000) *The Archaeology of Mediterranean Landscapes* (5 volumes). Oxford: Oxbow.

Binford, L. (1983) *In Pursuit of the Past: Decoding the Archaeological Record.* London: Thames and Hudson.

Boyle, R. (n.d.) 'Serendipity: how the vogue word became vague'. http://livingheritage.org/serendipity.htm

Fowler, M. J. F. (2004) 'Archaeology through the keyhole: the serendipity effect of aerial reconnaissance revisited', *Interdisciplinary Science Reviews* 29(2), 118–34.

Hodder, I. and S. Hutson (2003) *Reading the Past: Current Approaches to Interpretation in Archaeology* (3rd edition). Cambridge: Cambridge University Press.

Lloyd, G. E. R. (1973) *Greek Science after Aristotle.* London: Chatto & Windus.

Lloyd, G. E. R. (2002) *The Ambitions of Curiosity: Understanding the World in Ancient Greece and China.* Cambridge: Cambridge University Press.

Lock, P. and G. D. R. Sanders, eds. (1996) *The Archaeology of Medieval Greece.* Oxford: Oxbow.

McDonald, W. A. and G. R. Rapp, Jr, eds. (1972) *The Minnesota Messenia Expedition: Reconstructing a Bronze Age Regional Environment.* Minneapolis: University of Minnesota Press.

Maniscalco, M. L. (1998) 'Serendipity in the Work of Robert K. Merton', in C. Mongardini and S. Tabboni, eds., *Robert K. Merton and Contemporary Sociology.* New Brunswick and London: Transaction Publishers.

Merton, R. K. (1957) *Social Theory and Social Structure.* Glencoe, IL: The Free Press.

Merton, R. K. (2004) 'Afterword', in R. K. Merton and E. Barber, *The Travels and Adventures of Serendipity: A Study in Sociological Semantics and the Sociology of Science.* Princeton, NJ: Princeton University Press, pp. 230–98.

Merton, R. K. and E. Barber (2004) *The Travels and Adventures of Serendipity: A Study in Sociological Semantics and the Sociology of Science.* Princeton, NJ: Princeton University Press.

Piggott, S. (1989) *Ancient Britons and the Antiquarian Imagination: Ideas from the Renaissance to the Regency.* London: Thames and Hudson.

Remer, T., ed. (1965) *Serendipity and the Three Princes: From the Pereginaggio of 1557.* Norman: University of Oklahoma Press.

Renfrew, C. (1979) *Before Civilization: The Radiocarbon Revolution and Prehistoric Europe.* Cambridge: Cambridge University Press.

Snodgrass, A. M. (1987) *An Archaeology of Greece: The Present State and Future Scope of a Discipline.* Berkeley: University of California Press.

2 Understanding humans: serendipity and anthropology

RICHARD LEAKEY

I will begin this contribution on Serendipity by saying that whilst I know a lot of people I don't have very many friends. I do have a couple of friends to whom I spoke about this word serendipity, one of whom was French and the other French-Italian, and both assured me that there's no such word in their languages – and that if such a word does not exist in their languages it's obviously not a concept to worry about too much if you've got to prepare a paper on the topic. So I found that reassuring but I kept getting messages from Darwin College about how this topic was being addressed through all the different sciences of my co-contributors to the series, and it was obvious that it couldn't just be dismissed as easily as that. So I gave a lot of thought to it and I even moved myself to look it up in several English dictionaries and see what they said. But this didn't help at all in providing me with a direction because it increasingly looked like the sort of question I used to get at school that caused me to drop out. Questions that look easy but in fact are quite difficult – where first of all you not only have to know the answer but you have to understand the question – and then I really started to panic. So it is from this position that I start: at sea, but quite willing to have a shot at elaborating the role of serendipity in the story of our origins and in anthropology.

Let me begin by saying that I think it's important to be very careful not to get caught up with the notion, which serendipity might imply, that there's a faculty in evolution and anthropology to take advantage of chance. In the context of evolution what is it that could be said to have

Serendipity, edited by Mark de Rond and Iain Morley.
Published by Cambridge University Press. © Darwin College 2010.

that faculty? Is it the discoverer or the discovered that has been able to take advantage of chance changes and events?

We would not want to fall into the trap, that has been so hotly debated in Cambridge as a result of the work of Charles Darwin, of suggesting that there is a plan, design or a path that was always anticipated, so that when choices and chances arose organisms were somehow consciously or unconsciously able to use a faculty to say, 'Yes, it would be beneficial in terms of selection to take this option.' There is and will continue to be a tendency to somehow fall into that trap. On the contrary I take the position, perhaps best known through Richard Dawkins' explanation in his book *The Blind Watchmaker*, of suggesting that there is no such faculty in life (or life other than ours) that would drive our evolutionary choices in a conscious sense.

I think that there have been opportunities that have been exploited, however, and this is certainly something that I will discuss in terms of the main steps that I believe have been followed getting us to where we are today. But before I get to that I would like to take another tack: one which, again, we don't often think about. In the whole dispute about the evolution of our species that Darwin has taken credit for having started, there has been at times, particularly from the theological right, as opposed to the theological community, an assertion that these fossils that we find and we talk about don't add up to very much, and a question of whether it is really appropriate to use these few scraps of fossil bones to suggest such a departure from what used to be the received wisdom.

Obviously that situation has changed somewhat, but let's just talk about the fossil record for a minute and relate that to what I guess would be a common usage of the term serendipity as I understand it. Let's consider for a minute how absolutely remarkable it is that there are any fossils at all. The fact that there are so few is not the surprising thing — that there are any at all is astonishing. I'm afraid to say that your chance of becoming a fossil, I would wager, is about zero; it's a hard thing to have to accept, but it is. The chances of a natural living organism anywhere being fossilized are pretty remote and the chances of an early bipedal ape (or whatever we want to define it as) later becoming a fossil to be found by us when we are looking for them are remote in the extreme.

First of all when you die from whatever cause, you have to die some-where where there's a reasonable hope that your corporeal remains don't get consumed by scavengers: vultures, hyenas, sabre-tooth cats, lions and so forth. Furthermore we've got, and have had for millions of years, rather frail bones, which are to carnivores and depositional processes rather like chicken bones to cats and dogs – they can get crunched up terribly easily leaving nothing recognizable. You try looking at a chicken bone if the dog gets hold of it while your back is turned. There's nothing there that you could, after ten minutes, discern as having been a chicken. Not in my experience with my dog anyway. So surviving the various processes immediately post-death is pretty unlikely.

Then assuming that you've got over that hurdle, your bits are then lying around on the ground surface. They somehow have to be buried quite fast to stop them being destroyed by sunlight and rain and changing temperatures. This means that they have to get caught up in a sedimentary process where they get scrunched into the mud by other animals walking by or they get washed into the edge of a lake and get buried under the silt. So to go from stage one to stage two is in itself fairly unlikely, and once in the water, if the water has the wrong chemical balance the bones simply disintegrate very fast, the potential for preservation is gone and you have nothing.

So you have to get caught up in a sedimentary sequence where the soil is not too acidic and where there are the right elements in the soil for the process of calcification and preservation involved in forming a fossil to actually take place. Now that should not be taken as a given, but all those circumstances need to concur. So you get caught up in a sedimentary sequence which locks you safely away, but if the sedimentary area remains active, as many do, you gradually get covered by layers and layers of other sediments and your bones could end up several hundred if not a thousand metres below the present day surface. If you want to be found by a palaeoanthropologist it's no good being a fossil 1,000 metres underground.

So we can already see that being preserved at all is a pretty chancy affair, but then being found requires more than a little serendipity. Geological processes have to bring your sedimentary layer up again to the present day surface, through tectonic earth movement, earthquakes, tilting and erosion – all without destroying the fossils – and lo and behold several million years later these bits come back to ground level and lie around on the surface. Now, of course, they are subject once again not just to weathering and erosion but to the trampling feet of passing herds of animals such as goats, sheep, buffalo and elephants, and the chances of lying on the surface in the hot sun and remaining as intact as you were when you got buried are pretty slim. In fact, there's a pretty good chance that you won't make it.

Then on top of all that you've got to be found. You have to have come to the surface in an area where there's very little vegetation so that when your bits are lying on the surface to be seen by some fellow like myself or my colleagues, they're not covered with grass and leaf litter but they're actually there and you can see them and say 'look, there's an ancestor's bone' – which in itself requires sagacity.

Now, if you work out those probabilities of any one of us getting through that cycle, they're not very high, so the fact that we have any fossil hominid remains is astonishing; that we have so many, including almost complete skeletons, is absolutely incredible. We should recognize that in this sense there is an element of luck and exploitation of the opportunity which that presents, what you might want to call serendipity, that gives rise to a fossil record in the first place – and that's quite significant.

As I have implied above, I think that in evolution and palaeoanthropology the concept of serendipity has to be taken not from the standpoint of the discovered, but the discoverer. There are numerous ways in which that could relate to the processes of preservation and discovery, about all of which we cannot be sure, but we can be confident that the individual organism had no part in its fate in terms of turning up on the museum laboratory shelves.

If we approach serendipity from the point of view of the faculty of being able to recognize the opportunities inherent in a chance occurrence, this presents countless additional examples. In addition there are many fascinating examples of cases where exploitation of a certain opportunity has led to unanticipated benefits or further opportunities in a different direction.

But before we explore this from the point of view of the discoverer, in this instance we must also recognize that there are certainly cases in the biological process of evolution and adaptation that follow this model of unanticipated benefits. It is this which underlies the distinction made by evolutionary biologists between primary and secondary adaptations. This refers to the situation in which an organism may have adapted in a particular direction in response to a particular selective pressure (the primary adaptation), but as a consequence of this process actually accrues other advantages that weren't originally the purpose of the adaptation (secondary adaptations) that can then lead the organism in a totally different direction in terms of survival. We can come back to some of the many examples of that later in this discussion, but it is important to reiterate at this point that this is not to suggest that our ancestors and our forebears somehow had a faculty for selecting or choosing which way they wanted to exploit the circumstances that had arisen as a result of chance.

So let's come back to the whole issue of the discoverer. I know that in our family history there's been a great deal of credence given to Leakey's luck, and the idea that my parents before me, me subsequently and my wife and daughters who continue in the same field, have just been lucky. It's a nice thought that we're lucky, although sometimes it doesn't feel as if one's lucky. Of course, all these people have actually worked extremely hard and nobody talks about that part of the whole thing. And no matter how lucky we are, we're not going to find the complete skeleton of *Homo erectus* here on these green grass fields that are behind the colleges. Luck won't help you at all there.

So there have to be things that you can take advantage of, but you have to be in the right place and have the right attitude and ability to do so, and that's not necessarily luck. If you're better at taking advantage of a given opportunity than other people, maybe that's luck – I worry about it being luck, but maybe it's luck. In that sense we as a family have been extraordinarily lucky but I would put it down to the fact that we were in the right place at the right time with the right opportunities. I say to young students all the time that everybody in life sees many opportunities and most people in everyday life look at them going by and they say 'Wow, that's an opportunity' and then it's gone out the exit; then you hang around a bit and another one comes along and you smile and think 'there's another one, look', and it's gone. What my father told me was if an opportunity arises, grab it. If it stings or bites, well, then let it go and grab the next one, but don't let it get out until you know what it can do.

So I think that what people call luck is very much an element or characteristic of being willing to recognize and exploit opportunities. When you see opportunity, you should definitely take it and accept that there are high risks sometimes in doing so. In a sense it gets back to what serendipity was supposed to be about when it was coined back in the mid 1700s, emphasizing the role of sagacity in exploiting accidental occurrences.

So what are these opportunities? Well, one of the first examples I would give relates to my father and the path that led to him working in Africa. He was born in Kenya and he was long persuaded that East Africa, or Africa at least, would prove to be the birthplace of humanity, something that Charles Darwin had suggested, partly derived from the evidence for the Great Apes, the chimpanzees and the gorillas that live so broadly in Africa. It was not politically correct at that time to think of humans coming from Africa; you could have near-humans, *Australopithecus*, if you have to have something like that, but not humans. The success with which the Piltdown 'fossil hominid' hoax from Sussex was maintained for nearly 40 years (which was not, in fact, a very good hoax) owed much to this anathema of having African ancestors. Bad enough to have Asian ones, 'Java Man' and 'Peking Man' (*Homo erectus*), but now there's this fellow suggesting African ancestors; a good Brit would be much better not to look too closely at the evidence.

Now, as it happens, my father got into trouble and fell out with people in Cambridge and he took off in disgrace back to Africa. I think if he hadn't fallen out with people in Cambridge and had decided to make his career with an establishment wife and everything on received lines, I doubt very much whether he would have done all the things that he did in East Africa that led to these great discoveries and stimulated so many.

Is having a divorce, being precocious and being thrown out of college a form of serendipity? I'm not sure, but it may be, and is another aspect to think about. Certainly it was as a result of this that he found himself in a country with enormous opportunities to pursue archaeology and human evolution.

I was asked to speak very briefly at an opening ceremony in Cambridge in 2007 and I made the remark that my father, when he was at Cambridge as a student, was originally destined to become a student of theology and a cleric. His parents were very religious and believed very strongly that their offspring should follow in the Ministry. He was to be trained in the classics and theology and then go back and lead the masses to enlightenment through the teachings of Christ.

He wasn't, he said, very enthusiastic, but he was doing it as a diligent son. Then, playing in a practice rugby match for St John's College when they were trying to select University players, he got kicked in the head and got a serious skull fracture and concussion. When he came around and was obviously going to live, they decided that he should not think for a while. It's a rather nice treatment I would have thought. At that time a German expedition was going to what was then Tanganyika to collect fossil dinosaurs, and as a fluent speaker of Swahili he decided to apply for the job of interpreter. He got the job and went off with this expedition, and became absolutely riveted by the evidence for early life in the form of dinosaurs.

So when he came back, having thus mended his head sufficiently, he said 'No more of that clerical stuff – I want to go into archaeology and prehistory.' So he then changed his career dramatically as a result of the opportunity that he got when he observed fossil dinosaurs being collected by palaeontologists in Southern Tanganyika by a German expedition. So one might say that that was some aspect of serendipity playing its hand, if you like – a series of unanticipated events leading to unanticipated opportunities, which he then took.

He was apparently sufficiently popular with the German expedition that they offered him the chance to go back to Tanzania a few years later as a student and join them at the site of Olduvai, which was a known site with archaeology but little had at that time been found. So he went back and visited Olduvai for the first time in the late 1920s and became hugely impressed by the fact that there were bones of extinct animals from an erosion surface, mixed with what he took to be stone artefacts like hand axes – known at that time from Britain and France – of a type referred to as the Acheulean. So he decided that Olduvai was the place where the earliest creators of 'the Acheulean culture' lived, and that if he could find the remains of the maker of the stone tools living with extinct animals then he would have found the world's earliest man.

So he set his sails in that direction and got very much involved, purely as a result of these unanticipated events, chance happenings that were not pre-imagined or pre-planned, and followed that route.

My parents worked at Olduvai every year for two or three weeks, sometimes a month, under very difficult circumstances and very rarely found anything that lent anything to his ideas about human origins being there. But having got established there, in 1957 at one of the Olduvai sites, they found a nice big fat molar of an Australopithecus. He was convinced (as it happens he was probably wrong) that if there was one molar there must be a good number of others and they must be sitting in a piece of bone like a mandible (lower jaw) or a maxilla (upper jaw) and that therefore the thing to do now was to dig this place up, get his evidence and launch his career again.

So he persuaded an Englishman called Charles Boise to give him some money – it wasn't a lot of money, but they headed off. I remember very clearly them going off and saying, 'We're going to stay now and excavate the site and you'll hear we've got the big fellow, we've got the chap who made these tools.' But at that time I was 15 and in the last phases of my reluctant schoolboy years, and looking for other opportunities. My father had had the presence of mind to decide that he wished his anticipated discovery to be filmed, so he got in touch with the famous wildlife photographer Armand Denis, who lived in East Africa. Armand Denis knew my father and thought that if he really did make this discovery and he could get it on film then this would be a particularly important piece of Armand Denis' television. So Armand Denis arranged for his photographer, who was an Australian called Des Bartlett, to go down to Olduvai. By this point I was within a month of getting to the end of my final term at school and thought it was time I should leave anyway; the last month was just exams, so why not go early?

So I negotiated . . . well, I didn't negotiate, I just left, and joined this photographer and drove down to the site. We were delayed for three days on the way, so the excavation had to wait for us and my parents had to find something to do in the meantime. So in the three days' delay they sort of footled around, my father got sick and didn't go out much, and my mother went off looking in different places near where they were camped. This is when she discovered the skull of an Australopithecus. The day we arrived she'd made the discovery, so the next day they filmed the uncovering and it captured the world's attention. Now is that serendipity? I don't know, it was just one of those extraordinary things that happened, and had it not been for the film and the photography and the coverage it seems to me unlikely that the search for human origins at Olduvai, and later in other East African sites, would have got off to the start that it did. They didn't go back and excavate the other site for about ten years but focused on the site that they found when they were waiting for us. Nearby they found other sites and the whole saga of the discovery at Olduvai then took off. How much of that was Leakey's luck, how much was serendipity, and how much of it was just damned hard work, I don't know. But it was an extraordinary sequence of events that were all chance that resulted in this sudden opening up of a massive new interest in human origins in Eastern Africa.

Perhaps most importantly, because the National Geographic Society were involved in the making of the film, the publicity that it generated in turn generated funding and so the work continued. It's now just over 50 years since this discovery was made, the trigger that ultimately led to so much else contributing to our understanding of human origins in Africa.

I went up and started looking at Lake Turkana for fossils in 1968 and we were also very fortunate. The fossil hominids were sort of falling out of the rocks everywhere and we were in a very short time able to collect a significant number of important specimens. This was good for me because I had taken the initiative to go there, so was able to claim them as 'my' fossils and to say to my father and mother 'This is mine, don't give me your scientists, I will find my own scientists and lead this myself.'

I put together a team around me who were, of course, very willing to work with me because I had the best bones, and we had some magnificent years' work. What I would say is that again pure chance led to some incredible discoveries, but a very different kind of chance. I remember on one particular occasion we had found a mandible that was broken and there was a fair likelihood that we could find more of this mandible if we did some sieving, or screening, of the sediments. I set up a team of a few people to go out to the site and screen the sediments, who would be taken out by car in the morning and picked up in the evening. The site was right on the Ethiopian border and there was a certain amount of animosity between the Ethiopian tribesmen who were then there and the strangers (us) who were hanging around.

The team were busy collecting dirt and screening, and looking for these bits of bone, when several rifle shots rang out. They rang out not just as noise but like on the movies, with dirt being shot up in the air about two or three feet from where they were sitting. They didn't think this was at all humorous and decided they would return to the sieving later, and took to their heels. This was flat desert country, with very few places to hide, but there was a cliff about twenty feet high nearby, so they scrambled up that. Growing halfway up the cliff on a little ledge there was a big evergreen bush and they thought the thing to do would be get up there and get behind the bush where they could see what was happening but couldn't be seen, and they could then make some decisions what to do.

So they scrambled up this cliff as fast as they could, the three people, and hid behind the bushes. No more shots rang out and they never saw anybody, but they weren't quite as enthusiastic as they might have been to get back to work. It was hot and they were sort of sitting fiddling around, moving stones, and lo and behold there was another mandible. This turned out to be a very important find in the catalogue of discoveries, but nobody in their right mind would ever have gone up this cliff to hide behind the bush normally and we never would have found that mandible.

Now is that serendipity? I don't know. Is it luck? I don't know, but it was an unplanned consequence of another unplanned event that could have ended badly, but, in fact, ended extremely well – nobody got killed and we got a find of major importance that remains to this day one of the high points in those expeditions.

Let's then turn our attention to the other aspect of this question of serendipity in evolution, away from the discoverer to the discovered. What about these evolutionary events, these adaptations? How much

of this process is the same sort of thing? One of the big debates in palaeoanthropology that we're still talking about concerns the attainment of upright posture. Was this an exploitation of a previous adaptation or was there real selective pressure to become upright? How much can we say for the idea that we used to be four legged and knuckle walking like modern Great Apes, but that under selective pressure we started to use only our rear limbs to walk, meaning that we kept our hands free? We no longer used our wrists for support but started using our hands for other things, got the manipulative hands with our long thumb, and that this was somehow an indirect result of some other huge pressure that led to this sequence of changes?

Well, we don't know is the answer, and it is possible to speculate, but it's not impossible that we might yet find that there were other primates living elsewhere in Africa which, although already largely bipedal, hadn't taken the step that our ancestors took of actually using their hands for quite sophisticated purposes. One of the huge questions remaining today and one which undoubtedly is going to attract lots of research interest over the next decade or two concerns where and when this first happened. Did becoming upright happen once, only with our ancestors, or did it happen several times? One has to recognize that we know so little about the *origin* of bipedalism in the real sense that it's very hard to predict which way our understanding will go, and we need to recognize that there's much more to be discovered before we can fruitfully speculate on its origin.

Let's say, however, that there was a large ground-living primate that went around on two legs and had hands that were capable of picking up and manipulating things. We can seek to identify when this happened, but people might ask, does it really matter? On the one hand it seems to me that upright posture in a big-bodied ape may be the first reliable criterion for being on the human trajectory. On the other hand, as I recently commented in a discussion with some colleagues and students, the great mistake that was made at the beginning of investigations into human evolutionary origins was to suggest that we separated from the apes. This is what has generated all of the squabble about what really separates us and when a 'missing link' lived. It hasn't happened: we are the fifth ape and this ascension or descent from the apes is something

that maybe will happen one day but it hasn't happened yet – we are just another ape who does things very differently. If we'd have started off thinking about that we might have had far less contention in the story of our origins. On the other hand, of course, being perceived as separate from the apes was important if this idea of evolution was to be accepted, because allowing people to perceive themselves as being different from the apes was obviously important in those days 150 years ago when it was first a topic of frequent discussion.

So we're dealing with an upright ape. It was large-bodied, and seems to have been under pressure to survive, and it seems that there was some pressure to leave the deep forest cover. I say 'seems' because we don't yet know. But having hands that are no longer mainly occupied with supporting us as is the case with gorillas and chimps, and having fingers that as a consequence can be much more manipulative, this ancestor of ours started living a different way of life. At some point somewhere along the line meat became a particularly important part of the diet. Accessing meat is actually very difficult unless you've got big canine teeth or claws, neither of which our ape ancestors had. It's hard enough with something like a fresh rabbit, but if you get something up to the size of a dog or a deer, it's next to impossible to tear it apart with your bare hands unless it's putrid, and once it's putrid you may not want to do it.

Being able to access meat obviously had a significant survival value because meat is highly nutritious, it comes in convenient packages, and you can share it with others. There's a whole system of behavioural responses that you can relate to this. This is where the use of the stone tools comes in. We didn't get manipulative hands because we wanted to eat meat; we were able to access meat by making stone tools because we had manipulative hands, and we needed to do so because we had small teeth. The question is, is there any causal sequential relationship between when these different things occurred? Probably not, and this provides an example of a different set of behaviours becoming available through exploiting an earlier adaptation. The earlier adaptation of being bipedal gave rise to possibilities that were nothing to do with the original reasons for that adaptation. In these terms it may be possible to think of this as an example of serendipity in the process of evolution, although one still does

need to be very careful because we don't know exactly what the sequence was in which these events occurred.

But in any case we have got to a point in our story where we have an upright species with free manipulative hands, which was now gaining access to meat from carcasses because it could break stones and get a sharp edge to use. With meat it could do all sorts of things that it couldn't do before and, in particular, it could share food. If you've just got a few nuts or seeds you don't want to share them because it takes long enough to get enough to fill your belly let alone anybody else's. But if you can take a haunch of an animal that a lion killed, it's quite a reasonable package of food that you can share – so you can begin to show social behaviour patterns which we identify with being particularly human today.

But at this stage we are still small brained and still probably at what people would happily call the grunting phase, not particularly sophisticated in one's thinking, although quite how sophisticated we don't know. This state of affairs continues for a while, about half a million years, in fact, and then you start seeing not only crude stone tools but rather more sophisticated handaxes, and evidence that the brain is getting bigger too. The shape of the head changes as the brain gets bigger and the face gets smaller, becoming more orthognathic and less pronate, and there are lots of other changes that go on.

Why? Was this because we had a better diet? Was this because we were now selected for skills, with those who were slightly smarter getting more food, and raising bigger families and better? There's a whole series of circles that are probably interlinked in various ways that you can discuss until you're bored stiff, but we've yet to work out the answer. But what did happen was that that bipedal hominid using tools around 2 million years ago started to get a bigger brain. The brain went through further periods of growth and other periods when it didn't get much bigger and stayed stable, but what you do seem to see in the limited associated archaeological traces is evidence of a more complex lifestyle and social organization.

What has been very interesting in the last decade or two is that we've started to look in more detail at the life history and biology of these creatures. In particular it's important to think about the extended child-hood that we have. Our children, over the course of our evolution, have come to be born more and more as incompetent little things. They need a lot of parental care early on and they tend to stay longer with their parents because they're so incompetent – and in the process they learn a lot more from their parents. You can see in the developmental biology of some of the fossils of hominid infants that there have actually been some biological responses beyond just having a bigger brain.

What led to what? You have to be very careful not to get teleological in this kind of discussion but there is clearly evidence that some changes happened as a consequence of earlier changes, that weren't related to the original reason for those earlier changes.

So we have this fascinating story of becoming human, and right up to the point where you have a perfectly satisfactory human like us 200,000 years ago in Africa, it all seems to be going extremely well. They were not particularly sophisticated, but they were making tools and they had fire and they were hunting and collecting, and hominids of various types occupied much of the world.

And then apparently, if the geneticists are right and the evidence is right, some 65–70,000 years ago something else happened and suddenly there's a small population that gives rise to all of us modern people outside of Africa, whether we're from the southern tip of South America, central Australia, or Cambridge. We're all more or less closely related to a population that seems to have left Africa this side of 100,000 years ago.

What gave rise to this phenomenal change? What enabled some human group, virtually the same as everyone else but slightly different, to take over everybody else's territory and repopulate the world in place of all those who'd been there before? It wasn't a new biological species. Was it because we had a big brain? Well, we'd had a big brain for a long time.

I would guess it's probably related to a certain type of speech, in the sense of a form of language that makes it possible to talk about things that hadn't yet happened as well as things that had happened, and put all this in a context for planning purposes. It's quite useful to have that faculty to not just talk – and thus collectively think – about what you're going to do next but what you did before that might impact on what you should do next – in fact, talking about experiences is critical to the process of being human in the way that we are.

Then within a relatively short space of time, a few thousand years, some people, but not all, started domesticating animals and plants, living in one place, and making pottery and things like that. After a history of large-brained human ancestors going back a couple of million years, suddenly in the last 8,000 or 9,000 years people started carrying out these activities in particular ways which allow us to identify certain geographic centres in different parts of the world; and the behaviours became not just tied to settlements, but to settlements of sufficient size that you begin to get the roots of what we, in our part of the world, call 'civilization'.

So what happened? Why didn't that happen 20,000 years earlier? Why did it happen then and what is going to happen next? What is intriguing is that there are these events that we can identify archaeologically, allowing us to say in many cases *how*, but the question of *why* is a significant and very exciting part of the story that we can still tell.

As far as I'm personally concerned, the better understanding of anthropology and our origins is, if you like, now getting to the stage of being a detailed text. I think for the last 100 years, perhaps a little more, we've been really writing the headlines and some of the sub-headings, but we haven't really got into dealing with the text. It is today, with the interface of biochemistry and molecular biology, archaeology, ethology and animal behaviour, that we're really beginning to get a feel for what it was to be human or a human ancestor.

Clearly there have been sudden departures, which may have been triggered by events that, if you like, 'weren't anticipated' but have been beneficial, but I think serendipity plays a minimal role if any role at all in those events *per se*. It has, however, played a critical role in our discovering what those events were and how we've become what we are. As time goes on we will learn a lot more.

One of the last things I'd like to touch on is the intriguing issue of climate change. Today we're all very conscious of climate change, and clearly throughout this long story of human evolution the impact of climate on the various organisms involved has been critical. I don't think there's any doubt at all that the occurrence of climate change has played a far greater role in evolution and adaptation in terms of our own species than many of us give credit for; I think we're still in an age where some people consider climate change to be a matter that can be taken or left. In fact, I think what we're seeing is the onset of a process that could and will have huge implications for what happens to our organism as a species, and which we are accelerating. Modern, bipedal, thinking, talking, communicating humans are going to be impacted in a very dramatic way in a relatively short space of time.

Whether a short space of time is a decade or whether it's 100 years or 1,000 years, in terms of the span of several million years of our evolutionary history this will be very brief. We really need to pay much more attention to some of these issues and encourage the political leadership of the various countries from which we come not to play down the fact that we are a species that manifestly demonstrates that we have always been impacted by climate change – and there's absolutely no reason at all to believe that we won't be continually impacted by it.

Could this be the first time that serendipity could be deliberately brought to bear – using our faculty to sagaciously exploit chances and adaptations that we haven't thought about before? I think it could be, and perhaps some time in the future Darwin College will have another series on this theme and it will be recognized that finally serendipity has had a role to play in our success and survival as a species in relation to climate change.

Language is a technology and much of our modern technology is given over to communication – and perhaps serendipity could be considered to have had a role in our exploitation of these different types of technology. But a technology can be a double-edged sword. I do think that we have as a species been quite successful, not least through our ability to talk. Although too often while we do talk, we don't actually communicate, and this is a significant part of the problems facing us all today. I think one of the great failings of humanity is that somehow we haven't actually fully exploited our complex system of communication; maybe it's become too complex. A social insect like a termite or a bee gets the message and does as it's told. In contrast we don't get the message and very rarely do as we're told and that's led to many of the troubles that we face.

So to summarize, I'm a sceptic on serendipity in evolution *per se*. But I do think serendipity has, in the sense that it's used as an English word, played a huge role in the sequence of discoveries about our origins that I have described. It has impacted most dramatically on the discoverers, rather than the discovered. As one of these discoverers I can say that, as something of a rebel who dropped out of high school, I have tremendous fun taking advantage of all of the unanticipated opportunities that have arisen since.

3 HIV and the naked ape

ROBIN A. WEISS

Introduction

Dans les champs de l'observation, le hasard ne favorise que les esprits préparés.

Louis Pasteur, Lecture at the University of Lille, 1854

Pasteur's maxim that 'chance favours only the prepared mind' is as good a definition of serendipity as one can find. Serendipity has played an important role in microbiology, perhaps the most famous example being Alexander Fleming's discovery of penicillin. Microbes themselves, not being sentient, have no sagacity, yet they have been successful in seizing opportunities provided by chance to occupy new habitats such as the human body. As their name implies, microbes are small and they evolved on this planet long before plants and animals, but that does not mean that today's microbes are primitive, unsophisticated and survive only as curiosities or living fossils. Collectively, microbes represent the planet's largest biomass; they are essential in all ecosystems and they are the first living organisms to colonize hostile new environments. Microbes can be found in steaming volcanic springs, on Everest and in the depths of the oceans.

I shall confine my story to those microbes that invade the human body, and amongst them, to the subset of bacteria, viruses, fungi and parasites that causes disease, with an aside on a vector of disease – the origins of human lice. Where did humankind's infectious diseases come from and how have they influenced our genes and our societies? As I shall relate, some infections have co-evolved with us, others came from animal

Serendipity, edited by Mark de Rond and Iain Morley.
Published by Cambridge University Press. © Darwin College 2010.

sources, and some might possibly have come to *Homo sapiens* via other hominid species.

Evolutionary dynamics of host and microbe

Although humans share around 98 per cent DNA sequence similarity to our closest relative, the chimpanzee, at least 50% of our infections are different. Some of our infectious baggage has co-evolved with us since our separation from the great apes, whereas others have been picked up along the journey. When early humans emerged from the forest into the savannah and later moved out of Africa to occupy all continents, we acquired many kinds of infection which chimpanzees have never encountered, especially from the animals which we domesticated or which themselves chose to inhabit the human environment. However, very recent encounters with chimpanzees have also led to novel cross-species infections, notably of Ebola virus and human immunodeficiency virus (HIV).

In this volume, Richard Leakey discusses the serendipity of human evolution and I shall view humans as accidental hosts for agents of infectious disease. Our immune system remains much the same as that of other mammals, and it evolved to respond to a variety of infectious microbes. Therefore the specific list of infections matters less than the adaptability of the human or animal host to respond to them. Nonetheless, we are better adapted to control old infections than to handle new ones, which are more likely to become pandemic, that is, to spread uncontrollably through the human population.

Ancient infections have also given humans more time to evolve genetic resistance. Take malaria as a case in point. There are several examples of mutations in human genes that have been selected for increased resistance to the malaria parasite. These mutations mainly affect the phase of malaria propagation in red blood cells. Sickle cell anaemia, α- and β-thalassaemia, and glucose-6-phosphate dehydrogenase deficiency each cause severe disease in homozygous form (when we inherit the 'bad' gene from both parents), yet in heterozygous form (when we have one bad gene and one good gene) we show no genetic disease while it is difficult for the malaria parasite to thrive in red blood cells. The advantage of being resistant to malaria is so potent that the bad genes are sustained at relatively high frequencies in regions where malaria is or used to be rampant. Thus the selective advantage of resistance to malaria in the healthy carriers outweighs the death of their homozygous siblings. If both parents are carriers, the chances are that one in four offspring will die in childhood from genetic disease, whereas two in four will be resistant to malaria.

The CCR5 chemokine receptor serves as an essential receptor or gate on the cell surface for HIV to gain entry into T-helper lymphocytes and macrophages. A mutation deleting 32 base pairs in the gene for this receptor, known as CCR5Δ32, is prevalent in Europeans and it confers resistance to HIV infection. Since HIV has only been present in a small proportion of Europeans for one generation ($\sim$30 years), HIV itself cannot be the reason for the high prevalence of this genetic trait. It has been proposed by human geneticists that CCR5Δ32 may have been selected for providing resistance to smallpox or plague in the past, although there is scant evidence for this theory. I wonder whether an alternative selective force was possibly protection from rickets in high latitudes where there is little sunlight in the winter. Whatever the original reason for its selection, those who are homozygous for CCR5Δ32 are resistant to infection by the vast majority of transmissible HIV strains (and unlike sickle cell anaemia, the mutation itself is not harmful). Those who are heterozygous for CCR5Δ32 are less likely to acquire HIV infection and if they do, their progression to develop AIDS is delayed.

Working with Sunil Ahuja's group in Texas, we have recently identified another chemokine receptor that affects the risk of HIV infection. It is the Duffy antigen on red blood cells which serves as the receptor for the malaria parasite, *Plasmodium vivax*. The great majority of sub-Saharan Africans are Duffy negative and hence they are resistant to *vivax*. In contrast to CCR5Δ32, however, far from protecting them against HIV, it increases their risk of acquiring HIV by 40 per cent. We can attribute $\sim$11 per cent of HIV infections in Africa (amounting to 2.4 million infected people) to this susceptibility trait.

There remains a puzzle though. *Vivax* is not an ancient malarial parasite in Africa but arose in South-East Asia where it crossed the species barrier from macaque monkeys to humans. So what really exerted the selective pressure to make Africans uniformly Duffy negative? I suggest that it was the more virulent form of malaria, *Plasmodium falciparum*; yet this parasite does not need Duffy to enter red blood cells. My hypothesis is that *falciparum* did utilize Duffy in the evolutionary past but that as more and more humans in Africa lost Duffy, the parasite adapted to use an alternative receptor, glycophorin A, and took on a new lease of life. This anecdote illustrates that we have two opposing evolutionary processes going on, one in the host and the other in the parasite.

Since viruses and parasites reproduce more quickly than their hosts, they can outpace the host. With microbes, we can witness evolution happening in real time such as the development of antibiotic resistance in bacteria and anti-retroviral drug resistance in HIV. One may well question why infections do not kill the entire host population, but long-adapted, endemic infections tend to win a selective advantage by becoming less virulent. They therefore gain a longer window of time to spread to other hosts. This is particularly advantageous if the microbe is not highly contagious. Thus the reproductive rate of an infectious agent and its ease of transfer to a new host will play a role in determining its pathogenicity. However, this panacea of host and microbe developing a cosy symbiotic relationship over time leaves an unresolved puzzle, namely why increasingly selfish, more virulent variants do not take over the microbial population, rather like the emergence of cancer cells.

Humankind's collection of diseases

Let us examine the provenance of human infections as if they were a collection of paintings or furniture in a stately home, or perhaps in a Cambridge college. Table 1 shows a list of viruses. We can categorize the 'family heirlooms' as those viruses that have co-evolved with their host. Accordingly, the viruses most closely related to a human herpesvirus, cytomegalovirus say, are those of the chimpanzee, and then the bonobo, gorilla, orang-utan and so on. The evolutionary relationship between these viruses can be measured by analysing the sequence of their genomes and computing phylogenetic trees from these genetic sequences. With the family heirlooms, the phylogenetic trees of the viruses mimic the pattern of their hosts, even if the virus tends to diversify at a faster rate.

Many of the family heirlooms are acquired in infancy, like most types of herpesvirus; others may be passed sexually, like the papilloma virus

Table 1. *Origin of human viral infections.*

Family heirlooms (co-evolved with host)
Retroviruses
Herpesviruses
Papilloma viruses
Hepatitis B virus
Temporary exhibits (zoonoses)
Rabies
West Nile virus
Nipah virus
Ebola virus
SARS
New acquisitions (<12,000 years old)
Measles
Smallpox
Influenza
HIV

that causes cervical cancer. Some retroviruses have integrated into chromosomal DNA so that they are inherited as host Mendelian traits – about 8 per cent of human DNA represents 'fossil' retroviral genomes but they are not known to cause disease. Let us consider the herpesvirus, varicella-zoster virus. Upon primary infection, it causes chicken-pox; most infected individuals recover although they do not eliminate the virus altogether from their bodies. It remains present in latent form in sensory nerve cells. The virus can reappear later in life to cause shingles, which is a local eruption of chicken-pox, although most immune competent people keep the virus under control most of the time. An episode of shingles in a grandmother can set off a local epidemic of chicken-pox in children. Thus the persistence of the virus throughout the life of the host with sporadic re-activation ensures that it can be maintained indefinitely in a small, isolated host population, such as a group of hunter-gatherers.

Next there are the temporary exhibits. Table 1 lists five viruses belonging to different families that can infect humans but have not taken up permanent residence in us. They are 'on loan' from an animal reservoir and we call such infections zoonoses. For example, each human case of rabies comes from an animal, usually from being bitten by a rabid dog. The rabies virus has only five genes, but it manages to change its host's behaviour in a manner that promotes the spread of the virus. It induces aggressive behaviour at a stage of infection when copious amounts of progeny virus are secreted in the saliva. Untreated rabies is inevitably fatal in dogs and humans (though not in bats) so unless the virus is transmitted through biting, the virus also dies out.

Some zoonoses, however, manage to travel from person to person for a short period without setting up permanent residence in the human population. The SARS coronavirus spread rapidly from Southern China to Hong Kong and onward to Singapore and Toronto yet it eventually petered out. Some 877 people died from SARS infection in 2002/3, but then the outbreak ended as abruptly as it began. Humankind was lucky with SARS in that you do not become infectious to others until you are feeling really ill, absolutely rotten, whereas in the case of influenza virus infection, you are likely to cough and splutter for a couple of days before you decide not to come to work, which, of course, gives the virus a better chance to spread. When it does arrive, a new strain of highly pathogenic avian influenza to which we have no existing immunity could trigger a major pandemic killing tens of millions, as happened in 1918/19, but only if the virus adapts to efficient human-to-human transmission.

Let us move on, then, to our new acquisitions. These are the viruses that had a zoonotic origin, but adapted so successfully that they became self-sustaining in the human population. Now, by new I mean up to 12,000 years ago, as I would call that brand new on the evolutionary time-scale even though it takes us back to prehistoric times. Measles probably diverged from rindepest virus around 10,000 years ago, when we started rearing cattle and sheep. Since then the measles virus has evolved to become quite distinct from rindepest virus and it represents a virus that is usually transmitted only among humans. This means that neither it nor a precursor virus existed in chimpanzees. In fact, measles is highly dangerous to chimpanzees. Infections that are mild in humans may be lethal to the apes as they will have no natural immunity to that infectious agent. By analogy to zoonosis, we could call that an anthroposis.

Smallpox probably came to humans later than measles, not more than about 4,500 years ago, as far as we can gather from examination of mummies and other preserved human specimens. The closest animal relative to the smallpox virus is camelpox; the camel may well be its origin though some experts consider that both viruses may have come from rodents. Again, smallpox appeared in humans at a time when the human population was burgeoning after we had learned to domesticate and husband animals in the Fertile Crescent and the Nile Delta.

Influenza virus has repeatedly crossed from one host species to another. It now looks, from cloning and sequencing the H1N1 flu genome of the 1918/19 'Spanish flu' pandemic, that it was a pure avian strain which adapted to humans. On the other hand, the H3N2 influenza virus which first blossomed in humans in 1968 may have arisen as a genetic recombinant between an equine or porcine and an avian strain. As discussed later, the last virus listed in Table 1, HIV, first infected a human a little later than the Spanish flu, about 1930 if the molecular clock estimate is reliable.

I could have shown a list of bacteria rather than viruses, although not all the new acquisitions come from animals. Whereas all viruses are obligatory parasites and could therefore only have come to humans from animals, some pathogenic bacteria were free-living organisms before they found a safe haven in us. Bacteria closely related to cholera exist in rivers and estuaries; by a process known as horizontal gene transfer, cholera acquired genes for toxins and genes which helped it to adhere to and grow in the human gut. Cholera was first noted in 1815 in the Ganges–Brahmaputra Delta but it soon spread around the world, including the London outbreak in 1854. When John Snow showed that it was associated with water from the well in Broad Street, he famously removed the pump handle. Today, cholera is once again on the increase particularly in the favelas of South America.

Legionnaires' disease first broke out in a hotel in Philadelphia during a convention of the American Legion in 1976. This bug had adapted to live in the warm, moist atmosphere of modern air-conditioning systems, which are remarkably similar conditions to the human lung, and thus allowed it to become an infectious agent. Most bacteria, however, that have not co-evolved with humans come from animal sources, such as *E. Coli* O157, and the zoonoses causing Weil's disease or Lyme disease. But it is not always easy to determine which came first; for instance, bovine tuberculosis might have been secondarily derived in prehistoric times from the human form of the disease.

Globalization of human infections

Is the incidence of newly emerging infections increasing? There is no definitive answer to this question. We may have less exposure than we did in the past because the majority of us are no longer hunter-gatherers like Adam and Eve. Many of us who buy our meat at the butcher or supermarket have less close contact with our animal food sources than our forebears did. The separation of drinking water from effluent was a great advance in public health over a century ago, but it is threatened today by the growth of mega-cities in which most inhabitants live at high density in shanty-towns lacking basic sanitation. This year marks the point when over 50 per cent of the human population will live in an urban environment. When humans took to living in densely populated cities and engaging in crowd behaviour, such as going to football matches or on religious pilgrimages, human infections had a better chance of finding new hosts. That means that if a new virus emerged tomorrow, there would be a large enough pool of non-immune humans for it to adapt to become self-sustaining in us, especially if the infection is transmitted by the respiratory, oral–faecal or sexual routes. In addition, we have worldwide travel which is how SARS could travel from Hong Kong to Toronto so quickly.

It is instructive to look back at past periods of globalization to see just what happened concerning human diseases. *Yersinia pestis*, the plague bacillus, is endemic in Central Asian marmots, and can be transmitted to other species via fleas. In 1347/8 the Black Death depleted the European population by about one third. That pandemic would not have occurred if Genghis Khan had not conquered both China and the western steppes of modern Russia 150 years earlier. This in turn opened up the Asian Silk Road and the Genoese traders brought the plague back from Caffa, their trading post in the Crimea. It is said that the plague broke out among the Tartars who were besieging Caffa and that they catapulted corpses over the walls into the city. But it is likely that the rats, which carried the plague, found their way into the city too. The Genoese abandoned Caffa and took to their ships but the plague travelled with them. When they attempted to dock in Messina and Genoa the authorities quarantined the ships but black rats are agile at climbing down ropes. The Black Death succeeded to get onto European soil and soon spread rapidly.

The origin of syphilis is controversial. It may have been imported to Europe by Columbus because a related treponeme bacterium caused a disease known as pinta in Hispaniola. Alternatively, African yaws, a skin disease which is also closely related to syphilis, may have been brought back by Bartolomeu Dias and the Portuguese explorers. To date, genome analysis has not resolved which treponeme was the most likely precursor of syphilis. At any rate, syphilis was unknown in Europe before the late fifteenth century and was first documented in Barcelona in 1493. It was the Siege of Naples in 1495 that really gave syphilis a helping hand to become pandemic in Europe. Then, thanks to the Portuguese navigators, syphilis rapidly spread across the Indian Ocean to the Far East. Within a few years, the sailors travelling with Vasco da Gama and St Francis Xavier had brought syphilis round the Cape of Good Hope to Calicut on the Malabar Coast of India, on to Malacca on the Malay Peninsula, and eventually to Macao and Nagasaki. Thus syphilis and Christianity travelled together, by chance without sagacity.

In 1519, Hernán Cortés landed on the American mainland and within two years defeated the mighty Aztec empire. In fact, the Conquistadors were beaten back from the island city of Tenochtitlán, today's Mexico City, and they had to retreat to the mainland. But what did they serendipitously leave behind? – smallpox! When Cortés saw the pestilence that he had sown, he had the sagacity to return the following spring and conquer this devastated capital city.

During the ensuing 100 years it is reckoned by the historian and demographer William McNeill that the North American indigenous population fell by greater than 90 per cent. The population crash can be attributed to mumps and measles as well as to smallpox. They all played their part because these viruses had never been experienced by New World peoples. These viruses had spread from ruminants to humans in the Middle East within the last 10,000 years and the diseases had not reached the ancestors of the native Americans before they crossed the

Bering Strait. They were a totally naïve population with no herd immunity to these novel infections at all, and adults and children perished alike.

The knock-on effect of this implosion was profound. With too few indigenous people left to provide labour in the plantations the owners had to import them from elsewhere, creating a cruel though profitable slave trade. The pattern of population depletion due to the introduction of infectious diseases was repeated as Europeans explored South America, the Antipodes and the Pacific Islands. When we countenance the threat of new pandemics today, we should recall that Europeans have been net exporters of pestilence. Charles Darwin summed the situation up in 1838 in the notes he made during the voyage of the *Beagle*: 'Wherever the European has trod death seems to pursue the Aboriginal.'

While Cortés had the sagacity to capitalize on a chance event, later colonizers like Pizarro deliberately spread the deadly infections to natives. One of the best documented examples of ethnic cleansing by bio-weapons occurred in the Franco-British war in North America in the 1750s. The redcoat lieutenant-general Lord Jeffrey Amherst sent smallpox-contaminated blankets to 'Indian' tribes loyal to the French.

Jared Diamond has pointed out the lopsided nature of the 'Columbian Exchange' that followed the colonization of the Americas. The New World provided many plants to the Old World that soon became staple foods: maize, potatoes, tomatoes, peppers and so on. Unfortunately, tobacco was another West to East import. But with the possible exception of syphilis discussed above, all the infectious diseases travelled westwards. Diamond postulates that the small number of animal species domesticated by New World peoples, such as llamas and guinea-pigs, did not give rise to as many human infections, and that therefore the indigenous Americans had fewer infectious diseases overall. Chagas' disease is one of the few to emerge in South America. The trypanosome causing Chagas' disease is enzootic in South American rodents such as guinea-pigs. It infected European immigrants and it is now widespread in rats but it did not cross the Atlantic Ocean, perhaps because the blood-sucking bugs that are needed to transmit it did not get a foothold in the Old World.

Table 2. *Geographic origin of recently emerged human infections.*

- China: SARS and Avian Influenza
- Africa: HIV-1, HIV-2 and Ebola
- South America: Hanta virus pulmonary syndrome
- North America: Legionnaires' disease
- Malaysia and Bangladesh: Nipah virus
- Australia: Hendra virus
- Europe (UK): Variant CJD

Forecasting emerging infections

Table 2 illustrates that novel infections may arise in any part of the world and it is difficult to predict where the next one will appear. Wherever we look, on whatever continent, there are examples of emerging infections. In the UK we came up with our very own in the 1980s, mad cow disease (bovine spongiform encephalitis), because protein was extracted from the central nervous system of slaughtered cows and was incorporated into cattle feed. Cattle, of course, are naturally herbivores, and the imposition by humans of bovine cannibalism led to the spread of this novel prion disease. Sadly it became apparent in 1996 that it could spread to humans as variant Creutzfeldt-Jakob Disease. Forecasting the outbreak of new diseases is difficult, but if we are prepared to expect the unexpected (serendipity again), it might help us to respond more quickly and successfully, even if we do not know quite when and where it will emerge or what the nature of the agent may be.

The rate of environmental change may exacerbate the risk on encountering new infections. I shall cite infections emanating from fruit bats (flying foxes). Cut down a tropical rain forest and the fruit bats resident there can fly away to settle in orchards or trees providing shade around homesteads. Banana and papaya plantations offer attractive food to the bats which can spread their diseases in return. In 1998, the Nipah paramyxovirus of bats infected pigs in the eponymous village in Malaysia and the pigs in turn infected humans with lethal effect. More recently in Bangladesh, the same virus has infected humans directly. When the bats sample the fruit some of it falls to the ground and is contaminated by the bat's saliva. If children eat the fallen fruit more cases of Nipah virus disease occur, though luckily it has remained zoonotic and is not readily transmitted among humans. Hendra virus is related to Nipah virus and is present in Australian fruit bats. When a horse fell ill in 1999, the virus was transmitted to a stable-hand and a vet with fatal results. Neither Nipah nor Hendra viruses were known to virologists before these events occurred.

The SARS outbreak came from civet cats that were being imported into Southern China from Laos and Vietnam, to be served in restaurants as strong 'yang' bush meat in winter. Again, the natural reservoir of the SARS coronavirus appears to be South Asian fruit bats, from which it infected the civets. In Central Africa there have been several local outbreaks of Ebola virus from eating bush meat of butchered primates. Sluggish, sick animals are the most easy to capture and can spread the infection, but the long-term reservoir of Ebola is in fruit bats. Both insectivorous bats and fruit bats frequently harbour lyssaviruses, which are closely related to rabies virus. Daubenton's bats in the UK harbour European lyssavirus type 2; in 2002 there was a human case in Scotland after contact with a bat.

Most of our modern-day new infections originate from wild species, though domestic species such as chickens or pigs may act as an intermediate host and even as a 'mixing vessel' for recombinant viruses. The reason why novel outbreaks have an exotic origin is probably that we have had ample opportunity to pick up the standard infections resident in domesticated animals in the past. In addition, even if most individuals do not have intimate contact with wild fauna, a few intrepid exploiters of the environment can disseminate new infections rapidly once they cross the species barrier.

Origins of HIV

AIDS was first recognized in 1981 in the USA and the causative virus, HIV, was first isolated in Paris two years later. HIV had a zoonotic origin which can be extrapolated back to 1931, some 50 years earlier, to estimate the most recent common ancestor of the pandemic strain. The host to this common ancestor of the virus possibly represents the first infected human, or it might have been a bottleneck representing one infected individual some time after the initial transfer had occurred from a chimpanzee. The earliest blood sample that has proved in retrospect to be HIV positive dates from 1959 in Kinshasa in the Congo.

HIV has an 8–10 year incubation period from infection to the development of AIDS, so unlike acute infections like SARS or influenza, it could spread silently for many years before the new disease became manifest. We do not know whether HIV was as virulent 80 years ago as it is now and that AIDS deaths simply went unrecorded when they occurred, or whether the virus has hotted up as it became better adapted to human transmission. Chimpanzees which harbour the precursor virus, known as SIVcpz, may also succumb to illness. In the early years of HIV's sojourn in humans, it would have been a rare infection in a part of Africa where medical records were scarcely present.

Jonathan Heeney, who recently came to Cambridge as Professor of Veterinary Pathology, frequently discusses the mysteries of HIV's origins with me. We now know that even the precursor virus, SIVcpz, which is naturally resident in the chimpanzee, is actually a genetic recombinant virus derived from at least two other sources. Part of its genome is most closely related to an SIV strain in the red-capped mangabey and part of it to an SIV in the guenon, two different species of monkey. Somehow these two viruses recombined to form a hybrid virus either in the chimpanzee or in an unknown species before colonizing chimpanzees. The hybrid virus probably took some time to adapt in the chimpanzee and then needed to adapt again to humans. We do not understand exactly what it takes for a virus to adapt to a new species. Some infections are much more virulent in a new species and those are the ones we see and worry about, but some are so wimpy in a new species that we probably do not recognize the vast majority of them. Humans possess genes that restrict novel retroviruses from propagating in their cells, so part of the adaptation will be for the incoming virus to mutate to move around these obstacles.

The story is more complicated, however, and has been unravelled by Beatrice Hahn at the University of Alabama and Martine Peeters at the University of Montpellier. They collected faecal samples from wild apes and analysed the tiny amounts of viral sequences that they contain.

Their evidence indicates that HIV has crossed from the great apes to humans at least three times. The pandemic strain of HIV is known as HIV-1 Group M and has by now infected nearly 60 million people, some 25 million of whom have died as a result of infection. Group N has been detected only twice and each case may represent a person directly infected by a chimpanzee. Group O has spread from person to person and may have entered mankind about 10 years earlier than Group M, but it is not pandemic. It might possibly have come from a gorilla as both chimpanzees and gorillas have SIVs closely related to HIV-1 Group O.

We can assert three separate origins for HIV-1 because the genome sequence of each group is more similar to other ape viruses than they are to each other HIV-1. Group O is not known to have spread signifi-cantly outside its area of origin in Cameroon and neighbouring Gabon and Equatorial Guinea, except to one Danish sailor who came ashore at Douala and who died back home in 1966, some 15 years before AIDS was discovered. His disease seemed so outlandish at that time that his doctors wrote up it as a case report. The diagnosis of AIDS is with the wisdom of hindsight.

Such is the sophistication of modern-day 'forensic' DNA testing of different HIV and SIVcpz isolates that it is possible to map the origin of pandemic HIV-1 (Group M) to a small region in Southeast Cameroon where chimpanzees have SIVcpz with similar genetic sequences. Group M has diverged to comprise many subtypes labelled A–K in different parts of the world, and also recombinant forms between them. This high degree of variation is one of the stumbling blocks to developing an efficacious vaccine for HIV.

Quite independently from the appearance of HIV-1 in West Central Africa, HIV-2 appeared 3,000 kilometres away in the bulge of West Africa. HIV-2 has a different origin in sooty mangabey monkeys, not from apes at all. At least six separate transfers of HIV-2 have taken place, and two of them represent viruses associated with the eventual development of AIDS. However, HIV-2 is generally much less virulent than HIV-1 Group M.

We do not yet understand the precise mechanism of transfer of SIV to become HIV-1 and HIV-2. It is thought to be linked with the butchering of animals and blood borne infection. Neither do we know why the HIV

Groups differ so much in virulence, nor why all these transfers appear to be twentieth-century phenomena. Previous transfers might have taken place, but if they did they were not maintained in the human population.

If I were to think teleologically (which I shouldn't as an evolutionary biologist), then from HIV's point of view, crossing the species barrier from chimpanzees to humans is a wonderful piece of serendipitous good fortune. The original host, the chimpanzee, is a highly endangered species; it is likely to become extinct in the wild within the next couple of generations and thus SIVcpz would perish with it. By jumping across to humans to become HIV-1, the virus has ensured its survival. There are 6 billion humans and HIV-1 is thriving amongst us.

A lousy tale of the naked ape

The evolution of lice in relation to their hosts is as intriguing as viruses. In 1844, Charles Darwin wrote about lice in a letter to Henry Denny: 'What an interesting investigation would be the comparison of the parasites in representative birds of Britain and America.' If Darwin came back today, I imagine that he would be curious that the phylogeny of the lice infesting the great apes and humans is revealing some surprises. I shall briefly relate some recently published investigations of human lice undertaken by David Reed at the University of Florida and by Mark Stoneking at the Max Planck Institute for Anthropology in Leipzig.

Human head lice feed on the scalp and breed in the hair. We also have body lice which feed on the body but breed in clothing. Adam and Eve were naked in Eden and presumably did not suffer from body lice. Fifty years ago the eminent evolutionary biologist, Theodosius Dobzhansky, showed that body lice could adapt to become head lice. He concluded that although body lice are larger than head lice, they are variants of the same species. This interpretation is supported by recent analyses of several genetic sequences in the louse genome.

Stoneking estimated that body lice diverged from head lice about 100,000 years ago (his initial estimate was only 70,000 years but he extended it longer when he realized that the anchor sequence or outlier from which he calibrated his molecular clock was biased). He therefore suggested that we could estimate the approximate date of the origin of clothing to the period when body lice first appeared. More extensive recent data from Reed indicates that several clades (evolutionary branches) of body lice have spun off from head lice, and this observation would be consistent with more than one group of humans developing clothing, perhaps furs before fabrics were invented.

The animal louse most closely related to the human louse (*Pediculus humanus*) is that of the chimpanzee (*P. schaeffi*). The two species of louse diverged around 5.5 million years ago which roughly coincides with the divergence of their hosts. Thus human head and body lice would appear to be family heirlooms that co-evolved with us.

Interestingly, Reed discovered a distinct clade of *P. humanus* that was present exclusively in indigenous Americans and exclusively as head lice. He estimated that this New World clade diverged from the worldwide clade approximately 1.18 million years ago and has remained separate ever since. Since modern humans emerged only about 100,000 years ago, Reed postulates that the New World lice must have resided in a different hominid lineage for nine-tenths of the period since their divergence. The time of divergence fits well with the split between *Homo erectus* and the lineage that led eventually to *H. sapiens*. Thus we may have acquired the New World clade horizontally from another human species even though we did not interbreed with them. Given that we readily acquire viruses and parasites from apes and monkeys, it does not seem too far-fetched to accept Reed's hypothesis.

There is a third type of human louse that belongs to another genus altogether. This is the pubic louse (*Phthirus pubis*). These lice are often referred to as crabs owing to their appearance and they are well adapted to cling on to coarse pubic hair. It has been known for some time that the pubic louse morphologically resembles the gorilla louse (*Phthirus gorillae*). By analysing *Phthirus* DNA sequences, Reed has now shown that their phylogenies diverged around 3.3 million years ago. Since the most recent common ancestor of humans and gorillas was approximately 11 million years ago, it follows that the human pubic louse must have been acquired horizontally from gorillas or an intermediate host, perhaps at the time of the split of the *Phthirus* species.

This tale of lice illustrates that parasites can be useful indicators of human biology and evolution. There are several questions still to pose.

Might the era of pubic louse acquisition have been close to the time when human ancestors lost their body hair? Why did humans lose their body hair? Did we evolve through an aquatic stage as the zoologist Alister Hardy first postulated? Mark Pagel and Walter Bodmer have suggested that one selective advantage for being a naked ape was to be rid of body lice and to be seen to be free of them by prospective mates. And why, I would add, did naked apes develop pubic hair, which is not actually a feature of apes and monkeys? Since humans harbour two species of lice, have the other apes lost one lineage, or are we unusual in gaining a second? Are there other pairs of related parasites which humans have acquired horizontally, a theory put forward several years ago by Ashford?

Before leaving lice, it is worth remarking that all the kinds of human lice can transmit typhus, a disease caused by a tiny bacterium called Rickettsia. The reservoir of typhus is the rat and it can pass from rat to human via fleas. But once on board, it is more commonly transmitted from human to human by lice. It is called war fever and gaol fever because it often breaks out in the dire conditions that favour the breeding of lice. Typhus caused greater than 50 per cent mortality in Napoleon's Grande Armée of over 400,000 troops who set off for Russia (less than 70,000 returned). It was the most frequent cause of death in the Nazi concentration camps.

The impact of infectious disease today

My account of the various infectious diseases to which humankind is susceptible might give the impression that we are threatened for our very survival as a species, but that is not the case. Overall, the proportion of human deaths due to infections has greatly diminished over the past 150 years, while the mean life expectancy has risen. In the past 25 years, however, life expectancy has fallen by 20 years or more in parts of southern Africa largely as a result of the AIDS pandemic. Moreover, AIDS takes out mainly young adults rather than infants and the elderly, leaving grandparents to look after orphaned children. Therefore, as Richard Feacham illustrated in a Darwin Lecture last year, compared to other highly pathogenic infections, AIDS has an even greater social and economic impact on those communities where HIV is prevalent.

One infection can impact upon another. I discussed the genetic imprint an infection like malaria leaves on the human population earlier, but direct interactions between infections also occur. Ulcerative sexually transmitted infections such as genital herpes and syphilis increase the risk of HIV infection. In turn, the immune deficiency induced by HIV provides opportunities for infections to become rampant which would otherwise be kept in check. Thus AIDS patients present with zoonotic infections such as *Toxoplasma*, environmental agents such as *Mycobacterium xenopii*, fungal infections such as *Candida* (thrush), and reactivated family heirlooms such as cytomegalovirus and Kaposi's sarcoma virus. But the most deadly synergism is that between HIV and TB (*Mycobacterium tuberculosis*). TB is the most frequent opportunistic infection causing death in AIDS patients, but before the HIV-infected person dies, he or she may pass on virulent strains of tuberculosis to the general population.

Figure 1 shows a rough estimate of the annual mortality caused by certain infections compared to other causes of death, including natural disasters and human made calamities. These numbers represent a snapshot in time, for 25 years ago HIV would have been near the bottom of the scale and 65 years ago typhus would have been near the top. The major infectious diseases that were prevalent a century ago have been successfully controlled by two distinct public health measures: firstly, by improvements in sanitation and general living conditions; secondly, by the introduction of immunization.

Vaccines are our most effective weapons of mass protection. Smallpox has been eradicated as a naturally occurring disease and polio virus is now an endangered species. Children and adults can be protected from diphtheria, tetanus, pertussis (whooping cough), measles, mumps, rubella, hepatitis B and most recently, cervical cancer caused by human papilloma viruses. But sadly, there is still a long way to go before we shall be able to prevent malaria and AIDS through vaccination.

Conclusion

Naked apes are *nouveaux riches* regarding infectious diseases. Viruses, bacteria and parasites provide interesting clues about human genetic and social evolution. Several of these infections and infestations co-evolved

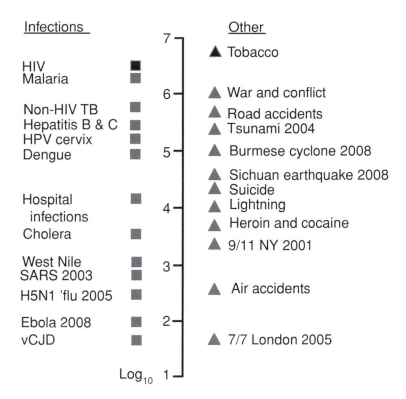

FIGURE 1. A 'Richter scale' of human annual mortality and some individual disasters. Where no year is shown, the estimated mortality for the year 2007 is shown.

with us but many others were acquired from domestic or wild animals, and some may even have been acquired from other human species. It is the new acquisitions that tend to cause the most severe pandemics such as influenza and AIDS.

Further reading

Diamond J. (1997) *Guns, Germs and Steel*. London: Jonathan Cape.

Feacham, R. and O. Sabot (2008) 'Surviving disease', in E. Shuckburgh, ed., *Survival*. Cambridge: Cambridge University Press.

Heeney J. L., A. G. Dalgleish and R. A. Weiss (2006) 'Origins of HIV and the evolution of resistance to AIDS', *Science* 313, 462–6.

Robin A. Weiss

Kittler R., M. Kayser and M. Stoneking (2003) 'Molecular evolution of Pediculus humanus and the origin of human clothing', *Current Biology* 13, 1414–17.

McNeill, W. H. (1977) *Plagues and Peoples.* Oxford: Blackwell.

Reed D. L., J. E. Light, J. M. Allen and J. J. Kirchman (2007) 'Pair of lice lost or parasites regained: the evolutionary history of anthropoid primate lice', *BioMed Central Biology* 5, 7.

Reed D. L., V. S. Smith, S. L. Hammond, A. R. Rogers and D. I. Clayton (2004) 'Genetic analysis of lice supports direct contact between modern and archaic humans', *PLoS Biology* 2, e340.

Van Heuverswyn F., Y. Li, E. Bailes, *et al.* (2007) 'Genetic diversity and phylogeographic clustering of SIVcpzPTT in wild chimpanzees in Cameroon', *Virology* 368, 155–71.

Weiss, R. A. (2008) 'Special anniversary review: twenty-five years of human immunodeficiency virus research: successes and challenges', *Clinical and Experimental Immunology* 152, 201–10.

Weiss, R. A. and A. J. McMichael (2004) 'Social and environmental risk factors in the emergence of infectious diseases', *Nature Medicine* 10, S70–6.

4 **Cosmological serendipity**

SIMON SINGH

While writing a book about the Big Bang, I was shocked at the role played by serendipity. Lucky astronomers who just happened to be at the right place at the right time seemed to make the biggest breakthroughs. In particular, radio astronomers were relentlessly struck by good fortune. I had always laboured under the impression that hard work, diligence and prolonged genius were the keys to success, but instead it seems that great discoveries are often the result of happy accidents.

For example, in 1930 the American Telephone and Telegraph (AT&T) Corporation was employing Karl Jansky to work out what was causing the crackling interference on their transatlantic radio-based telephone service. He built a giant, highly sensitive radio antenna and mounted it on a turntable that rotated three times each hour, allowing it to pick up radio waves from all directions. When Jansky's back was turned, local children would perch on the struts of the world's slowest carousel, which is why the antenna was nicknamed 'Jansky's merry-go-round'.

Jansky soon spotted that the radio interference could be classified in three ways. First, there was the distinct impact of local thunderstorms. Second, there was a weaker, more constant crackle from distant storms. Third, there was an even weaker form of interference, which Jansky described as 'composed of a very steady hiss type static the origin of which is not yet known'.

In due course, careful analysis of the timing and direction of this mysterious hiss eventually proved that it was coming from the heart of our Milky Way galaxy, where intense magnetic fields were interacting with fast-moving electrons, resulting in a constant output of radio waves.

Serendipity, edited by Mark de Rond and Iain Morley.
Published by Cambridge University Press. © Darwin College 2010.

Jansky had become the first person to show that astronomical objects could emit radio waves, a truly historic discovery that ultimately led to the discipline of radio astronomy. In other words, astronomers realized that they could use radio telescopes, as well as optical telescopes, to study the universe. It encouraged astronomers to look beyond visible light and use the entire spectrum as a tool for exploring the cosmos.

Jansky announced his result in a paper entitled 'Electrical disturbances apparently of extraterrestrial origin'. The story was picked up by the *New York Times*, which ran a front-page article on 5 May 1933, which included a reassurance to readers: 'There is no indication of any kind . . . that these galactic radio waves constitute some kind of interstellar signaling, or that they are the result of some form of intelligence striving for intergalactic communication.' Nonetheless, this did not stop a pile of letters landing on Jansky's desk claiming that he was receiving important messages from aliens that should not be ignored.

Jansky's detection of galactic radio emissions is a perfect example of serendipity, inasmuch as he had stumbled upon something wonderful that he was not looking for in the first place. As outlined in the introduction to this book, the word 'serendipity' was coined in 1754 by the politician and writer Sir Horace Walpole, who had read a fairy tale called *The Three Princes of Serendip*. He explained in a letter to a friend that the princes 'were always making discoveries, by accidents and sagacity, of things which they were not in quest of'. An alternative definition was given to me by a scientist, who said that serendipity was like looking for a needle in a haystack and finding the farmer's daughter.

The history of science and technology is littered with serendipity, so much so that I was able to present six programmes for BBC Radio 4 entitled *The Serendipity of Science* and wrote weekly columns on this subject for the *Independent on Sunday*. The radio series and the columns included famous examples of serendipity, such as the discovery made in 1948 by George de Mestral when he went for a stroll in the Swiss countryside. He saw some prickly seeds on his trousers, noticed that their spiny hooks had got caught on the loops in the fabric, and he was thus inspired to invent Velcro. In another example of sticky serendipity, Art Fry was trying to develop superglue when he accidentally concocted a glue that was so weak that two pieces of paper that had been stuck together could easily be pulled apart. Fry, a keen member of his local church choir, coated bits of paper with his failed superglue and used them to flag pages in his hymnbook, at which point the Post-it note was born.

I also included some examples of medical serendipity. For instance, Viagra was initially developed as a treatment for heart problems, but when it was subjected to clinical trials it was found to have no significant impact on such conditions. The disappointed researchers abandoned the trial and asked patients to hand back their unused pills, but they were surprised that there was an extreme reluctance among many of them to return the pills. Thus the real benefit of Viagra was discovered by accident.

Another example of medical serendipity concerns the development of the cataract operation. Surgeons had tried to remove an opaque lens and replace it with a glass lens, but experience had shown that it was inevitably rejected. Dust or sand on the surface of the eyeball can cause enormous irritation, so it is not surprising that a foreign object inside the eyeball is problematic. However, in the 1940s one British eye-surgeon, Harold Ridley, encountered several fighter pilots who had suffered eye injuries caused by the splinters from shattered cockpit canopies. Spitfire pilots in particular seemed to suffer from canopy splinters embedded in their eyeballs. Ridley noticed to his surprise that these splinters did not cause any severe problems. They sat quietly in the eye without causing inflammation and without being rejected. The reason for this was that the canopies were made of perspex, a material that is so inert that the eyeball accepts it. This inspired him to develop a plastic lens, which in turn allowed successful cataract operations.

Returning to radio astronomy, serendipity not only gave birth to this new observational technique, but also played a central role in several discoveries. For example, 40 years ago, in February 1968, the scientific journal *Nature* announced a serendipitous discovery in a paper entitled 'Observation of a rapidly pulsating radio source'. A team of Cambridge astronomers were using a radio telescope when they accidentally spotted an object emitting a regular burst of radio signals. Jocelyn Bell, the PhD student who initially made the discovery, dubbed the signal LGM-1, which was an abbreviation for Little Green Men 1. It was later identified as a new type of pulsating star, or a pulsar. These rotating stars emit beams of radiation in opposite directions, and these are only detectable when they sweep past us, rather like a lighthouse beam (this is discussed further by Andy Fabian in his chapter).

Another serendipitous discovery in radio astronomy occurred during the Second World War, when the schoolteacher Stanley Hey was asked to address a particular problem that was confronting Allied radar operators. Their radar screens occasionally lit up like Christmas trees, preventing operators from identifying enemy bombers among the multitude of signals. The assumption was that German engineers had developed a new radar jamming technology based on directing radio waves at British radar stations. However, Hey noticed that the jamming appeared to be coming from the east in the morning, from the south around lunchtime and from the west in the afternoon, and then stopped at sunset. Clearly this was no Nazi secret weapon, but merely the result of radio emissions from the Sun. By researching radar, Hey had accidentally become the first person to detect solar radio waves.

Hey seemed to have a knack for serendipity, because in 1944 he made another lucky discovery. In order to spot incoming V-2 rockets, he had developed a special radar system pointed up at a steep angle. But while looking for rockets, Hey showed for the first time that meteors also emit radio signals as they sizzle through the atmosphere.

Hey was a pioneer of radio astronomy and doubly serendipitous, yet he did not make the greatest accidental discovery in radio astronomy. That honour goes to an American pair who would by sheer chance use radio astronomy to prove the veracity of the Big Bang model.

In the 1960s, Arno Penzias and Robert Wilson were working at AT&T's Bell Labs, where Karl Jansky had invented radio astronomy thirty years earlier. Although Bell Labs was a commercial research facility, it still encouraged some pure research, so Penzias and Wilson received permission to spend some of their time scanning the skies to study various celestial radio sources. They used the 6-metre horn radio antenna, sited at nearby Crawford Hill, which had originally been designed to detect signals from the innovative Echo balloon satellite. Government intervention in this sector of the communications industry persuaded AT&T to withdraw from the Echo project, leaving the horn antenna free to be transformed into a radio telescope.

Before they could do any serious surveying, Penzias and Wilson first had to fully understand the radio telescope and all its quirks. In particular, they wanted to check that it was picking up a minimal level of noise, a technical term used to describe any random interference that might obscure a genuine signal. In radio astronomy, the signals from a distant galaxy are so feeble that the issue of noise is paramount. To check the noise level, Penzias and Wilson pointed their radio telescope at a part of the sky devoid of radio galaxies, a region where there should be virtually no radio signals from space. Anything that was detected could then be attributed to noise. They fully expected the noise to be negligible, so were surprised to discover an unexpectedly annoying level of noise. Although the noise level was disappointing, it was not so high that it would seriously affect the measurements that they were intending to make. Indeed, most radio astronomers would have ignored the problem and embarked on their survey. Penzias and Wilson, however, were determined to conduct the most sensitive survey possible, so they immediately set about trying to locate the source of the noise and, if possible, reduce it or remove it completely.

Penzias and Wilson surveyed the landscape for any spurious noise sources, and even pointed the telescope towards New York, but there was no increase or decrease in the noise. They also monitored the noise level with time, but again the noise was continuous. In short, the noise was absolutely constant regardless of when and where the telescope was pointed.

This forced the duo to explore the possibility that the noise was coming from their own equipment. Penzias and Wilson checked every single element of the radio telescope, looking for dodgy contacts, sloppy wiring, faulty electronics, misalignments in the receiver, and so on. At one point, attention focused on a pair of pigeons that had nested inside the horn antenna. Penzias and Wilson thought that the 'white dielectric material' deposited by the pigeons and smeared on the horn might be the cause of the noise. So they trapped the birds, placed them in a mail van and had them released 50 kilometres away at another Bell Labs site in Whippany, New Jersey. They scrubbed the antenna until it was bright and shiny, but alas the pigeons obeyed their homing instinct, flew back to the telescope's horn and started depositing white dielectric material all over again. Penzias captured the pigeons once more, but this time he reluctantly decided to get rid of them for good: 'There was a pigeon fancier who was willing to strangle them for us, but I figured the most humane thing was just to open the cage and shoot them.'

Despite a year of checking, cleaning and rewiring the radio telescope, the annoying noise continued. What the two frustrated radio astronomers had not realized was that they had stumbled upon one of the most important discoveries in the history of cosmology. They were completely oblivious to the fact that the omnipresent noise was actually a remnant of the Big Bang: it was the 'echo' from the early expansion phase of the universe. This annoying noise would turn out to be the most convincing signal that the Big Bang model was correct.

Back in the 1940s, the American physicists George Gamow, Ralph Alpher and Robert Herman made some calculations about conditions in the early Universe. They showed that the very, very early Universe would have been a seething mess of protons, electrons and photons, with the photons (or light particles) bouncing off the charged protons and electrons. After some expansion and cooling, however, the Universe would have undergone a transition – the cosmos would have calmed down sufficiently for the electrons and protons to bond and form hydrogen atoms, whereupon the photons would have stopped their relentless scattering. This is because photons are much less likely to scatter off neutral combinations of particles.

This would have allowed the photons to flow through the Universe largely unimpeded, giving rise to a blast of radiation filling the entire Universe, and this radiation would be a direct consequence of the Big Bang. The trio of theorists had predicted that this afterglow of the Big Bang should still be present throughout the Universe. They also predicted that the radiation would have originated as a very short wavelength, but the expansion of the Universe would have stretched the waves so that they would appear today in the form of microwaves, a type of radio wave. Unfortunately the technology did not exist to detect this so-called cosmic microwave background (CMB) radiation, so the prediction was soon forgotten. Furthermore, this was a period when few people believed in the Big Bang theory, so nobody else believed in these speculations about the CMB radiation. And this is also why, over a decade later, Penzias and

Wilson failed to make the link between their radio noise and the predicted Big Bang radiation.

To their great credit, Penzias and Wilson refused to just ignore the mysterious radio noise and remained distressed and perplexed. They continued to discuss it between themselves and with their colleagues, and eventually news of the microwave hiss reached a cosmologist who was able to point out the true significance of these observations. Suddenly, everything fell into place. The omnipresent noise had nothing to do with pigeons, dodgy wiring or New York, but instead it had everything to do with the creation of the Universe.

Even before Penzias and Wilson published their research, the story reached the general public on 21 May 1965 thanks to a lead front-page story in the *New York Times*, which carried the headline 'SIGNALS IMPLY "BIG BANG" UNIVERSE'. This was such compelling evidence in support of the Big Bang model of the Universe, that this effectively marked the moment the Big Bang became widely accepted as a true description of the origin of our Universe. A more formal and official acceptance of the Big Bang took place over a decade later when Penzias and Wilson received the 1978 Nobel Prize for Physics.

And yet all this was the result of sheer luck. Penzias and Wilson's success relied wholly on being blessed by serendipity. The CMB radiation was just waiting to be discovered by anybody who happened to point a sufficiently sensitive radio antenna at the cosmos, and by chance that turned out to be Penzias and Wilson. However, the serendipitous nature of their discovery was nothing to be ashamed of, because such breakthroughs require not only luck but also considerable experience, knowledge, insight and tenacity.

For example, there is strong evidence that the Frenchman Emile La Roux in 1955 and the Ukrainian Tigran Shmaonov in 1957 both detected the CMB radiation during their radio astronomy surveys, but they both shrugged off the apparent noise as a minor defect in their instruments that they were prepared to tolerate. They lacked the sort of sheer determination and doggedness that allowed Penzias and Wilson to discover the CMB radiation.

So it would be unfair to label serendipitous scientists as merely lucky. Indeed, they are only able to build upon their chance observations once they have accumulated enough knowledge to put them into context. As Louis Pasteur, who himself benefited from serendipity, put it: 'Chance favours only the prepared mind.' Also, those who want to be touched by serendipity must be ready to embrace an opportunity when it presents itself, rather than merely brushing down their seed-covered trousers, pouring their failed superglue down the sink or abandoning a failed medical trial.

Perhaps the best spin on serendipity comes from Winston Churchill. He once observed: 'Men occasionally stumble over the truth, but most of them pick themselves up and hurry off as if nothing had happened.' In contrast, Jansky, Hey, Penzias and Wilson all stumbled on the truth, and all of them were stopped in their tracks, unable to ignore the profound implications that confronted them.

5 Serendipity in astronomy

ANDREW C. FABIAN

Astronomy is an observationally led subject where chance discoveries play an important role. A whole range of such discoveries is continually made, from the trivial to the highly significant. What is generally needed is for luck to strike someone who is prepared, in the sense that they appreciate that something novel has been seen. 'Chance favours only the prepared mind' in the words of Pasteur (1854).

This is one definition of serendipitous discovery, first identified as such by Horace Walpole in a letter in 1754 to Horace Mann on discussing a Persian tale of three Princes of Serendip. Several more interpretations[1] are outlined in these chapters, but I shall stick with the concept of a chance or unplanned discovery. In contrast with school laboratory science where the aim is to plan and carry out an experiment in controlled conditions, in general astronomers cannot do this and must rely on finding something or a situation which suits. Often, the possibilities afforded by a phenomenon are only appreciated later, after the surprise of the discovery has worn off.

A nice example is the discovery in 1979 of the volcanoes of Io by Voyager 1 (Figure 2). This phenomenon was spotted by a navigational engineer, Linda Morabito, rather than one of the project scientists. Io turns out to be the most volcanically active body in the Solar System.

'Chance favours only the prepared mind' implies both an element of luck and a prior understanding of what is normal. Making successful discoveries in astronomy is not comparable to buying a lottery ticket and then sitting back but requires a deep familiarity with the Sky, the Universe, cosmic

[1] See e.g. *The Travels and Adventures of Serendipity*, Merton and Barber 2004

Serendipity, edited by Mark de Rond and Iain Morley.
Published by Cambridge University Press. © Darwin College 2010.

FIGURE 2 NASA image of Io showing active volcanoes.

phenomena and/or physics. It does require both sides; you don't make discoveries without making observations and you don't identify them as such without knowing when something is new. As some examples from chemistry clearly demonstrate, some clumsiness, or at least a deviation from what would otherwise be the path of best practice, may also be needed (mercury was discovered to be a catalyst for synthetic indigo when a mercury thermometer was broken in the reaction vessel; Roberts 1989). It may not prove easy to build algorithms or robots to make serendipitous discoveries!

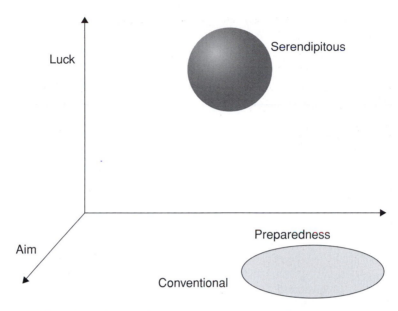

FIGURE 3 Serendipitous discoveries combine luck (or chance), preparedness and aim.

I am sure that chance plays a strong part in the way in which we learned the world as children. Playing is just that and we all start out with curiosity outweighing prejudice. Only later, alas, does prejudice come to dominate and become the enemy of discovery. It must have played an important role in the development of astronomy and science. It is possible, of course, to continue to make serendipitous (if not original) discoveries oneself, such as why the full moon always rises at sunset.

An illustration of how I define serendipity is shown in Figure 3. The axes of this three-dimensional figure are luck, preparedness and aim. Pure serendipity lies just on the luck–preparedness plane, whereas the perfectly planned, Kantian (Glashow 2002) experiment is just on the preparedness–aim plane. In reality many serendipitous discoveries have some aim (Archimedes was surely thinking about the problem of estimating the volume of an irregular object when he stepped in his bath), and I shall allow that. There just has to be a large unexpected element.

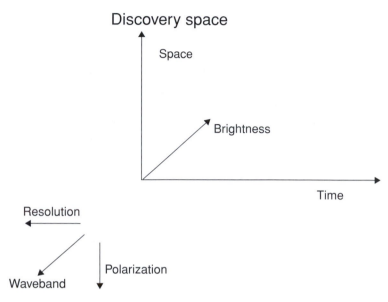

FIGURE 4 A schematic representation of some parts of Discovery Space.

One way to categorize discoveries is through Discovery Space (Figure 4; Harwit 1981). New things are generally found when new parts of Discovery Space are explored. We need to go more than about three times deeper in that space to find new things. Discovery Space is multi-dimensional and not just in space and time but in spectral band (e.g. radio vs. visible), spectral resolution (discerning different frequencies or colours), time resolution, polarization etc. A familiar analogy to a multi-dimensional space is provided by our senses; hearing is distinct from smell or sight and if we make them more acute we discover new things. Imagine having the sensitivity to smell of a dog, or the sensitivity to electrical activity of a shark!

Serendipity often involves an element of surprise, which implies an emotional quality to scientific work. Like a good joke which leads in one direction before jumping to another, so a serendipitous discovery – a Eureka, or even a 'what the . . .' moment can jump our train of thought to new directions. The way in which a serendipitous discovery turns our thoughts, either individually or collectively, into new directions is one of the major benefits of serendipity.

Note that discovery doesn't always make you famous. Stigler's law of eponyms states that 'no scientific discovery is named after its original discoverer' and indeed Stigler did not discover that law either. It is also worth stressing that there is lots of noise or spurious signals in most observational searches so it pays to become very familiar with the instruments and how they work.

Astronomy is powered by serendipitous observations and serendipity is an accepted mode of progress. There are hundreds of research papers with 'serendipitous' in the title and I found 17 in 2007. One theme which I shall develop is that although serendipity is part of astronomy it is not directly factored in to the decision or funding processes to the extent that it might successfully be. Science's outside appearance of being rational and methodological is somewhat at odds with serendipity. There is a tension associated with it and a 'fishing expedition' is a derogatory term used by time assignment and funding panels. This may be a legacy of our innate feeling that serendipity is somehow obvious, random or childish.

I have spent much of my career in X-ray astronomy, which had a serendipitous beginning. Indeed, X-rays were discovered serendipitously by Röntgen in 1895. We are all familiar with X-rays for their property of being easily absorbed by the bones of our body. The astronomical X-rays mostly observed by astronomers are even more easily absorbed and can only travel a few inches in air. Consequently, X-ray astronomy must be carried out above the Earth's atmosphere from high-altitude balloon, rocket or satellite. Solar X-rays were discovered in the 1950s (see Friedman 1991) but it was estimated that it would be impossible to detect the X-rays from other stars using the equipment of the time. Riccardo Giacconi proposed to NASA using a sounding rocket to look for solar X-rays reflected from the Moon. In a short rocket flight on 18 June 1962 he and his team discovered diffuse X-ray emission from around the Sky and a peak of emission in a direction which did not point at the Moon. They had found Sco X-1 and the X-ray Background (XRB). We now know that the first is due to matter from a normal star falling onto an orbiting neutron star; the XRB is due to matter falling into distant supermassive black holes.

Unexpected discoveries are routinely made in astronomy, even sometimes by amateurs. The NASA website Astronomy Picture of the Day,

which is one of the first things I log into each day, has most of them
and can certainly be appreciated by everyone. A recent example, Comet
Holmes, first discovered in 1892, flared up by a factor of 500,000 last
November and was first spotted by J. A. Henriquez Santana in Tenerife
as a naked-eye object in the constellation of Perseus. Why it flared up
is still a mystery, although the list of possible reasons is growing. It
is unlikely to have been due to a collision with something else since it
probably did the same abrupt brightening when it was discovered. It must
have an inherently unstable core; presumably it briefly had much stronger
'volcanoes' than Io. Such events in the Sky must have been familiar to
the Chinese and Korean court astronomers who watched the Sky as a
way to predict the future of both the Emperor and the State. Some of
the events they witnessed were supernovae, which mark the collapse and
subsequent explosion of stars. One such led to the expanding supernova
remnant known as the Crab Nebula (Figure 5) (it doesn't really look like a
Crab, but then the constellation of Cancer doesn't either). We now know
that the solid remnant of the collapsed star is a neutron star spinning
at 30 times a second. Neutron stars were predicted to exist in the 1930s
soon after neutrons were discovered in Cambridge. They have the mass
of the Sun but a radius of just 15 kilometres, which is smaller than
London. Long suspected to be the power source of the nebula, the
object was not identified as such until after pulsars were serendipitously
discovered by Jocelyn Bell, Antony Hewish and others in 1967 (Bell
Burnell 1983).

They were looking for the flickering of so-called radio stars, due to
the solar wind, in order to determine how small they are (the effect of
turbulence in our atmosphere on the visible light from stars which are
pointlike makes them twinkle, whereas planets which are extended do
not). They built an array of aerials sensitive to variations of a second
or less. Jocelyn Bell discovered 'scruff' every sidereal day on the pen
recorder charts within which 1.3 s pulses appeared. Little Green Men
as the responsible agent were ruled out when several more pulsars were
found. They are rapidly spinning, highly magnetized neutron stars. The
Crab pulsar is just one of many, but played a key role in developing the
theory of how they operate since the nebula acts as a calorimeter for
the power radiated.

Crab Nebula ▪ M1   *HST* ▪ WFPC2

NASA, ESA, and J. Hester (Arizona State University)   STScI-PRC05-37

FIGURE 5 The Crab Nebula.

Interestingly the pulsar was suspected to be the energy source before (it was known as Baade's star). I've heard stories that the occasional lay observer saw the object twinkling (their eyes may have been particularly sensitive to variations). X-ray data of the Crab taken just before the Cambridge radio discovery of pulsars was later found to show pulses but, and this is important, was not analysed in a way that revealed the pulses at the time (Fishman *et al.* 1969). How many important discoveries are lying in someone's archive or hard disk?

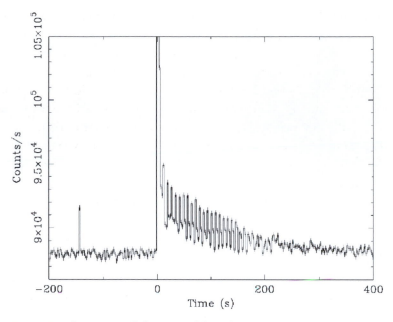

FIGURE 6 Gamma-ray light curve of the soft gamma-ray repeater SGR1806 from December 2004.

Sometimes, supernovae mark the formation of a black hole, which can produce intense, brief, gamma-ray emitting jets seen as a gamma-ray burst (GRB). Observations of GRB have been dominated by serendipitous discoveries from the very start when seen by US military (Vela) satellites in 1967 and announced in 1972. Some are observed right across the Universe and are the brightest things in the Universe during their brief life. Some GRBs are different and are due to quakes on neutron stars with superstrong magnetic fields, 1,000 times stronger than those of a typical radio pulsar and several thousand million million times stronger than the Earth's magnetic field on earth. Such objects are called magnetars and a recent outburst on 27 December 2004 from SGR1806 gave the strongest event ever observed at any wavelength (Figure 6). For the first two-tenths of a second the (mostly gamma-ray) energy flux on Earth received from this object, which is about 30,000 light years away, exceeded that of a full moon. It was then intrinsically 1,000 times brighter than the 100 billion stars in our Milky Way galaxy! It saturated all gamma-ray detectors and some of the best measurements of its maximum brightness came from a Russian satellite instrument which was in Earth's shadow and saw the emission reflected from the Moon. The decay phase of the event consisted of 5 sec pulsations which were even detected as oscillations in Earth's magnetic field (the gamma-rays ionized the upper atmosphere which in turn affected the magnetic field). If astrologers wanted to have a scientific basis for their 'predictions' they would take up gamma-ray astronomy. If the event had been much closer then it could have profoundly affected us all – in a very negative manner.

The time domain is the least explored one in astronomy and continues to be rich in discoveries. It is likely to be opened up further over the next decade with telescopes mapping the visible Sky every few days such as Pan-STARRS, LSST, Lofar, Gaia, SKA etc. Such instruments will produce vast amounts of data (many Terabytes) every day so analysing the data will be a serious challenge. This is becoming an issue with the enormous facilities now coming on line in many subjects. The Large Hadron Collider is an example from physics. So much data is produced that most has to be eliminated immediately. How to optimize such enormous data gathering exercises for serendipitous discoveries is unclear.

Sometimes the object or effect was predicted earlier, but considered too faint or difficult to be seen. This was the case with both neutron stars and black holes which are so tiny that it seemed reasonable to assume that they would be unobservable. What was required was for the emission to be stimulated (as in a laser) for the pulsar or highly beamed by relativistic outflow for the GRB. Any scientific paper written predicting their observational detection well before they were discovered would rightly have been rejected!

The discovery of the black hole at the Galactic Centre is a further example of this. While not exactly a serendipitous discovery, it was made possible by the lucky, and still unexplained occurrence of suitable markers (the He stars) in that place. Two teams, one led by Genzel in Munich the other by Ghez in Los Angeles, have seen and followed the motion of individual bright stars orbiting the central black hole. One star has now been seen over the past 15 years to complete one whole orbit. The precision with which this elliptical orbit has been measured leaves us in no doubt that the central 4 million solar masses of our Galaxy are extremely compact and can only be a black hole.

One effect of gravity is to bend light. This was first measured for the Sun during a total solar eclipse by Cambridge astronomer Arthur Eddington in 1919. It matched Einstein's predictions and is what made Einstein famous. Further examples were lacking for almost 60 years during which time few people considered the effect from an observational point of view. Then in 1979 a double quasar[2] was discovered by Walsh, Carswell and Weymann, who were making routine measurements of the properties of a large sample of quasars. Two of the quasars were separated by 6 arcsec and were found to have identical spectra. So identical that at first they didn't think that the telescope operator had actually moved the telescope. What they had discovered was light being deflected above and below a massive galaxy along the line of sight. When things are exactly lined up the background source appears as a ring (an Einstein ring) around the lensing galaxy (Figure 7), but in a more typical case such as the double quasar where things are slightly mismatched then the image appears as two separate objects (a third one occurs at the centre but is often absorbed by dust in the lensing galaxy). Both images of the double quasar vary with what we now know is the same pattern yet shifted in time by 430 days, which is the difference in light travel time along the two paths. Gravitational lensing has now become (and remains) something of an astronomical industry. More dramatic examples were found in clusters of galaxies in the 1980s (Figure 8). Again these were found serendipitously. They had certainly been seen earlier (and can be seen in published images) but not noticed as such.

One of my own serendipitous discoveries is of ripples in the hot gas at the centre of a cluster. To observe the gas requires X-rays and the image was taken with the Chandra X-ray telescope (Figure 9). The ripples correspond to quasi-spherical ripples in the pressure of the gas. They are strong sound waves created by the action of gas accreting into the supermassive black hole at the centre of the central galaxy of the cluster. There are several notable properties of these sound waves, the first is that they carry lots of energy to large radii, in essence they enable the

[2] A quasar is an accreting massive black hole producing so much radiation that it outshines its host galaxy.

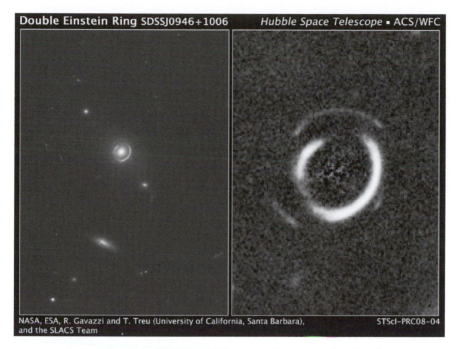

Double Einstein Ring SDSSJ0946+1006 | Hubble Space Telescope ▪ ACS/WFC

NASA, ESA, R. Gavazzi and T. Treu (University of California, Santa Barbara), and the SLACS Team   STScI-PRC08-04

FIGURE 7 A double Einstein ring caused by gravitational lensing.

central black hole to have a significant influence on gas over intergalactic distances, the second is that they have a very low frequency of one ripple per 10 million years! It corresponds to a B flat about 57 octaves below middle C. The main response of the UK media to our press release on this was just the B flat!

As my final example I return to our Galaxy to discuss the case of extrasolar planets, which were long sought for but only found orbiting normal stars in 1995. (Curiously, three planetary-mass objects were found orbiting a pulsar in 1991.) The problem lay in everyone's expectations which supposed that other solar systems would resemble our own. In our own Solar System the most massive planet, Jupiter, orbits far out every 12 years creating a very tiny response in our Sun which would be difficult to measure in other stars. In the first extrasolar system found, it was a Jupiter-mass planet in a 4-day orbit! Being so close means that its effect on the star is much larger than if it were in a 12-year orbit, swinging that star about at 60 rather than 12.5 m per sec (Figure 10). Such 'hot jupiters'

FIGURE 8 Galaxies in a rich cluster, the total mass of which is
gravitationally bending the light from distant galaxies into many arcs.

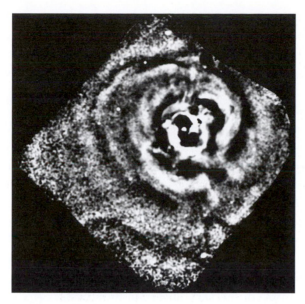

FIGURE 9 Chandra X-ray image of the centre of the Perseus cluster of galaxies.

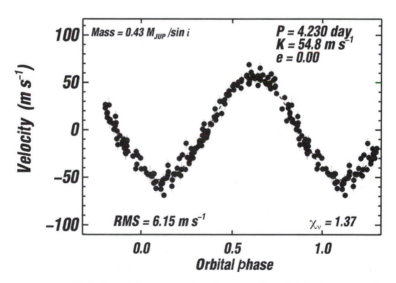

FIGURE 10 Velocity of the star 51 Peg along our line of sight (courtesy of G. Marcy).

give a much larger signal than anyone had expected. Now hundreds have been found, not all with such extreme orbits, but nevertheless few of them actually resemble our own (many of much more highly eccentric orbits than found in our Solar System). 55 Cancri is the nearest one with five planets.

This leads me to an area of research in astronomy which relies solely on serendipity, namely the search for extraterrestrial intelligence. What are the chances of detecting another intelligent civilization? Drake's equation gives us some idea. The number of civilizations, N, in the Galaxy with which we can communicate is given by $N = Rf_p n f_l f_i f_c L$, where R is the rate with which stars are being formed (about 1 per year), f_p is the fraction of stars which have planets, n is the number of those planets which are habitable and f_l, f_i and f_c are the fractions of those planets on which life, intelligence and communicable civilizations occur. L is the lifetime in years of a communicable civilization. The detection of extrasolar planets has pinned down one of the very uncertain numbers, f_p (to say 10 per cent or more). Even then the optimist will find that $N \sim 0.001 - 0.01 L$. A key unknown is the length of time a technologically aware civilization lasts, L. Ours is only just over 100 years old and we need them to last millions of years for N to be in the 1,000s or more. If they do last that long then we are most likely to find a civilization in the middle of its run, not just near the start as we are. Therefore we will be dealing with civilizations which are hundreds of thousands to millions of years more technologically advanced than our own.

If so, then what will they look like and how will they communicate? Would our present methods seems as absurd for interstellar communication as smoke signals would do across continents? Should we look for highly directed radio signals, which is where the effort has gone so far, or maybe for flashes of X-rays or gamma-rays, as I suggested 30 years ago (Fabian 1977)? Won't any intelligent civilization be looking for serendipitous flashes in the night?

It is clear that astronomy is rich in serendipitous discovery and phenomena. Harwit predicted that such discoveries would soon slow down as most things were discovered. His argument was based on the assumption that the phenomena have equal weight but given that they are not I foresee such discoveries continuing on well into the future. Several of my examples have been drawn from the past few months and years and even then I had a wide range of discoveries to choose from. In many areas, astronomy is still in an exploratory discovery phase. Cosmology too is equally rich, as is discussed by Simon Singh. In the near future we can expect surprises from neutrino and gravitational wave astronomy. We may yet find that dark matter, which comprises 21 per cent of the Universe, comes in 42 different varieties.

Does it not then make sense to tailor our research funding, both for the hardware – the telescopes – and for the modes of working, to take this into account? This leads to a current dilemma. Facilities (and people) are increasingly expensive. Funding agencies using public funds want value for money so are most likely to fund projects and telescopes and teams where a successful outcome is predicted. This tends to mean looking into areas close to where we know, rather than stepping out into the unknown. In the case of serendipitous discovery there is little that can be predicted with certainty, we can only argue on the basis of past success. It means stepping out boldly in discovery space.

This situation contrasts with laboratory physics where experiments are mostly controlled and conditions predictable. This is not to say that serendipitous discovery is then absent, as is discussed by Richard Friend, but when a new facility costs millions to billions of pounds then it is generally the clearest defined case with predictable outcomes which wins the money. The situation with respect to astronomy has become polarized by an emphasis on fundamental physics in some quarters. In that view, how a galaxy works is of less interest than the more fundamental issue of whether there are or are not other dimensions to space, for example. Astronomy is often tied up in the messy complexity of everything, whereas the 'fundamentalists' want to study the (assumed) much cleaner basis of it all.

My own view on this is that since fundamental physics has not made significant discoveries since 1979 (Smolin 2007) then a direct approach on the fundamental problems may not be the best. If there are other dimensions, they could as well emerge from some serendipitous astronomical discovery. When looking at the night sky with the naked eye, averted vision is often best, and an averted, rather than directly focused approach to discoveries can often pay off best. We have to keep observing

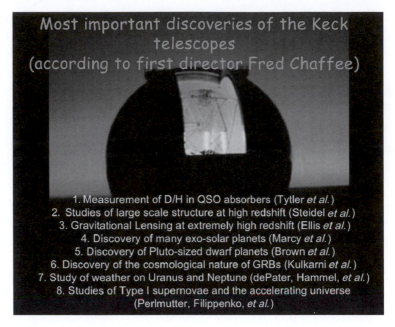

Most important discoveries of the Keck telescopes
(according to first director Fred Chaffee)

1. Measurement of D/H in QSO absorbers (Tytler *et al.*)
2. Studies of large scale structure at high redshift (Steidel *et al.*)
3. Gravitational Lensing at extremely high redshift (Ellis *et al.*)
4. Discovery of many exo-solar planets (Marcy *et al.*)
5. Discovery of Pluto-sized dwarf planets (Brown *et al.*)
6. Discovery of the cosmological nature of GRBs (Kulkarni *et al.*)
7. Study of weather on Uranus and Neptune (dePater, Hammel, *et al.*)
8. Studies of Type I supernovae and the accelerating universe
(Perlmutter, Filippenko, *et al.*)

FIGURE 11 Some Keck discoveries.

the Universe in all its detail – general astronomical observatories of all wavebands are the way to go.

This 'fundamentalist' debate is not settled (e.g. White 2007) and will continue to play out over the next decade. It is ironic that our telescopes are remembered mostly for the serendipitous discoveries they made (Keck, Hubble Space Telescope) (Figure 11) and not for the issues for which the original science case was made, yet we put most of our efforts into the known science aspects of the science case for a new telescope. Rather like the common view of democracy, or peer review, this common approach is highly flawed but is however the best available.

References

Bell Burnell, J. (1983) 'The disovery of pulsars', in K. Kellermann and B. Sheets, eds., *Serendipitous Discoveries in Radio Astronomy*. Greenbank, WV: NRAO, p. 160.

Fabian, A. C. (1977) 'Signalling over stellar distances with X-rays', *Journal of the British Interplanetary Society* 30, 112.

Fishman, G. J., F. R. Harnden and R. C. Haymes (1969) 'Observation of pulsed hard X-radiation from NP0532 from 1967 data', *Astrophysical Journal* 156, L107.

Friedman, H. (1991) *Astronomer's Universe: Stars, Galaxies and Cosmos.* New York: Ballantine Books.

Glashow, S. L. (2002) http://physics.bu.edu/static/Glashow/barcelona2002.html

Harwit, M. (1981) *Cosmic Discovery: The Search, Scope, and Heritage of Astronomy.* New York: Basic Books.

Merton, R. and E. Barber (2004) *The Travels and Adventures of Serendipity.* Princeton, NJ: Princeton University Press.

Roberts, R. (1989) *Serendipity: Accidental Discoveries in Science.* New York: Wiley.

Smolin, L. (2007) *The Trouble with Physics.* London: Penguin.

White, S. D. M. (2007) 'Fundamentalist physics: why dark energy is bad for astronomy', *Reports on Progress in Physics* 70, 883.

6 Serendipity in physics

RICHARD FRIEND

I think I was asked to give the lecture on which this chapter is based because it is widely known around Cambridge that we made an unexpected and important finding in my research group in early 1989. Our 'Eureka moment' was the finding that thin films of an organic polymer (long chains of covalently bonded carbon atoms) designed to behave as a semiconductor could emit green light when sandwiched between two metallic electrodes with a DC current passed through them. We had made a polymeric light-emitting diode and, unusually among discoveries in physics, it was very easy to see that it worked! We had dozens of students and staff drop by the laboratory to see those diodes glow – brightly enough to see them clearly through the windows of the vacuum chamber we used to keep them away from air. The whiteboard in the laboratory soon acquired some artwork to celebrate the event (Figure 12).

Carbon-based electronics

Carbon sits just below silicon in the periodic table and the two elements therefore show some properties in common. The world of semiconductor technology settled on silicon in the early 1960s and silicon has, of course, supported a remarkable and unexpected industrial revolution, still progressing at breathtaking speed according to Moore's Law. Carbon supports much more complex chemistry than silicon, and Nature uses the limitless range of carbon-based molecular structures to support life. Some of Nature's molecules are highly coloured so that they can capture the energy in sunlight; retinal is deployed to absorb light

Serendipity, edited by Mark de Rond and Iain Morley.
Published by Cambridge University Press. © Darwin College 2010.

FIGURE 12 Foreground – weak green light emissions from an early polymer light-emitting diode (c. 1989) enclosed in a vacuum chamber; background – laboratory whiteboard with artwork attributed to Karl Ziemelis (copyright University of Cambridge and Karl Ziemelis).

in the eye, and molecules such as chlorophyll and carotene are used in green plants to absorb light and convert it to chemical energy. The early stage processes in both vision and photosynthesis resemble the processes involved in silicon semiconductor devices, so we had set out to investigate whether carbon-based molecules or polymer chains could be 'wired up' to electrodes and made to work analogously to silicon.

Our first success had happened a couple of years earlier when we demonstrated that Field Effect Transistors, FETs, could be made with a related polymer, polyacetylene. We were very fortunate to have been first to get access to a material synthesized by Jim Feast and his colleagues in Durham. Polyacetylene is impossible to process once made because it is insoluble in most solvents and cannot be melted. The Durham group had devised an elegant method to get round this problem, making a soluble 'precursor' polymer that could be processed from solution to form films that are then converted in situ (through the loss of a side-group under mild heating conditions) to leave the polyacetylene film in place. We used this process to construct FETs as illustrated in Figure 13. Our transistors were not particularly good as transistors go; they switched only low currents because the gate field induced charges in the polyacetylene layer were not very mobile. However we had made them for another reason: although polyacetylene does show silicon-like properties, the mobile electronic charges present on the polymer chains when the transistor is switched on behave very differently. Rather than behaving just as free particles, they carry with them a rearrangement of the carbon–carbon bond lengths that introduces a topological excitation or solitary wave. This had been predicted to carry with it an electronic energy level that is neither bonding nor antibonding in character, sitting therefore in the middle of the energy gap between filled (valence) and empty (conduction) states. We set out to find this new energy level by detecting new optical absorption produced by optical transitions between the conduction or valence states and this new 'mid-gap' state, and Jeremy Burroughes duly found it (at an energy of about 0.7 electron volts) by measuring the modulation of a reflected optical probe beam as we modulated the transistor gate voltage (Burroughes, Jones and Friend 1988). Some ten years later, the performance of polymer transistors was developed to the point where these could be used as transistors and they now show real promise, as I discuss below.

We wanted to use some other semiconducting polymers besides polyacetylene in our transistors, and therefore tested one of the few other film-forming polymers, poly(phenylenevinylene), PPV. In early 1990 we had access to it through our recently established collaboration with Andrew Holmes in the Department of Chemistry. He and Paul Burn synthesized this material – in contrast to polyacetylene (which to the eye is metallic black), PPV is yellow-green and highly fluorescent. We had great difficulty in getting it to work in a transistor (though we did succeed some years later), but in the course of testing its conductive behaviour, Jeremy Burroughes made some simple sandwich structures in which a layer of the PPV polymer was sandwiched between two metallic electrodes, as illustrated in Figure 14. He noticed that when the voltage was raised high enough for a current to be passed through the polymer layer, its characteristic yellow-green fluorescence could be seen through

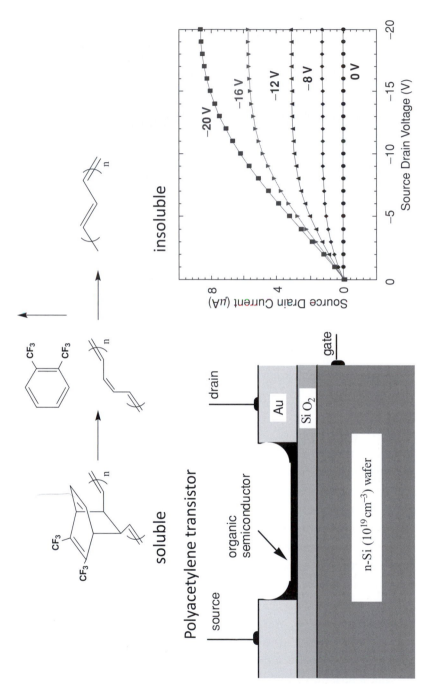

FIGURE 13 Top left: the Durham route to polyacetylene. Bottom left: FET structures formed with polyacetylene. Bottom right: transistor switching characteristics (copyright University of Cambridge).

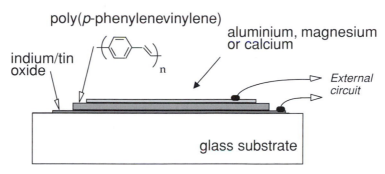

FIGURE 14 Polymer light-emitting diode structure (copyright University of Cambridge).

the top electrode of aluminium that was, fortunately, thin enough to be semi-transparent.

We realized that this was an important observation, and Jeremy Burroughes, Donal Bradley and I did have the sense to file a patent that allowed us to get worldwide protection for light-emitting diodes made with any semiconducting polymer, before we published (Burroughes *et al.* 1990). This pitched us into the engineering and commercialization of this early-stage technology and to the formation of Cambridge Display Technology.[1] The ability to coat large areas with arrays of our light-emitting diodes by, for example, ink-jet printing, can be exploited to construct large-area television screens. Though the liquid-crystal display is currently the dominant display technology, organic light-emitting diode displays are intrinsically more energy-efficient, are faster and brighter, and have the potential to be cheaper to manufacture.

Research in physics

In asking when progress in scientific research is the result of serendipity, we perhaps presume that the mainstream development of science is not. I disagree with this presumption – most of the big breakthroughs in physics have been and continue to be unplanned and unexpected. The public projection of big science projects, such as the Large Hadron Collider at CERN, has, however, been misleading. The popular media present

[1] See website at www.cdtltd.co.uk

the particle physics community as though it knows where the next big problem is. Thus many new big experiments have clear preset objectives, such as that of the Large Hadron Collider, which was constructed to find the Higgs boson. This is not how I saw science when I started my career in research, and the evidence I have accumulated since then supports my position. The unexpected will continue to set the agenda.

The brief account (above) of my research with carbon-based semiconductors reveals that I work in the broad field of 'condensed matter', or 'materials' physics. Materials are very complex – usually far removed from systems that can be treated exactly using established laws of physics. Just occasionally, their complexity seems to be unimportant and we are able to describe properties with simple and almost intuitive models. Thus, we like to describe the movement of electrons within semiconductors and metals as though they are free particles travelling around as if they do not interact with one another (though they must, because they are electrically charged and repel one another strongly). We push these simple descriptions as far as we can, with great success. Often, however, these models fail unpredictably, sometimes with spectacular consequences. I discuss later the science (and sociology) of the phenomenon of superconductivity in metals, which depends fundamentally on interactions between electrons. Found in many metals at low temperatures, this is associated with the complete loss of resistance to the flow of electrical current and is an example where quantum mechanics presents us with a phenomenon that is completely outside our everyday perceptions of the physical world. To discover new properties that reveal fundamental physical laws is the stuff of alchemists' dreams, and the prospect of fame and fortune in the field of superconductivity makes an interesting story that I think is relevant generally.

Planning a career in serendipitous physics

The jungle within which scientific research takes place must now seem daunting to those setting out in their careers. We operate in an increasingly accountable world, where there are strong pressures to produce short-term benefits, so setting out to find the unexpected, in an area where short-term results are unlikely, seems to be a dangerous course to take. I thought it might therefore be useful to set out some 'advice' for the younger researcher planning a career.

Rule 1   Look for technology outside the field

Technology generally precedes science. I know this is uncomfortable reading for fellow scientists, but the evidence is clear. The telescope with which Galileo found the moons of Jupiter was made possible by the availability of lenses developed for use in spectacles. J. J. Thomson succeeded in 1897 in identifying the electron as a fundamental particle, just ahead of several European competitors, in part because he happened to have a better vacuum pump that allowed electrons in his cathode ray tube to travel far enough to be measured before colliding with residual gas molecules. The technology that was developed in industry to purify, process and manufacture semiconductor devices based on silicon or gallium arsenide enabled the discovery of new quantum states for electrons confined to travel two-dimensionally within a plane in the presence of a magnetic field – the Quantum Hall Effect and the Fractional Quantum Hall Effect. I could develop a very long list, but would emphasize that many of the important examples are very recent.

TECHNOLOGY FOR LOW TEMPERATURE: THE DISCOVERY OF
SUPERCONDUCTIVITY

Superconductivity in metals provides a good working example. Simple gases had been a very important area of study at the end of the nineteenth century. Besides nitrogen and oxygen there are also small quantities of the inert gases in the atmosphere; Lord Rayleigh had found the first of these, argon, in 1894. It was important to connect their properties to the other states of matter, liquid and solid, and this required technology to separate individual gases and cool them to a low enough temperature so that they would liquefy or form a solid. By the end of the century, James Dewar and others had scaled up production of liquid oxygen and liquid nitrogen. This requires that the gases are cooled to 200 °C below room temperature, and though cold, this is still 70 °C (to be correct, 70 Kelvin) above absolute zero and is not so difficult to reach. There are, however, more obstinate gases for which the intermolecular attractions needed to form the liquid phase are weaker, so that the boiling points are correspondingly lower. In 1898 Dewar succeeded in making liquid hydrogen which boils at 20 K above absolute zero, but his technology was not adequate to liquefy helium, the remaining challenge. This was accomplished by Kamerlingh Onnes in Leiden in the Netherlands in 1908, at a temperature of 4.2 K above zero.

Metals are so familiar to us that we fail to realize how strange they really are. Their ability to conduct electricity, and therefore to reflect light, results from some of their valence electrons being decoupled from regular chemical bonds so that they are free to move throughout the solid and carry an electrical current. Whether this behaviour would persist at very low temperatures was, in Onnes' days, unclear. At such a low temperature, random thermal motion of the atoms in the solid is very substantially frozen out and if the motion of electrons from one site to the next requires a little of bit thermal energy to overcome a small barrier, then maybe electrons should slow down and stop as temperature falls (as might be expected from the Third Law of Thermodynamics). But these same thermal motions of the atoms are responsible at high temperatures for limiting the distance that electrons can travel before being scattered, hence limiting their conductivity, so that cooling the metal raises its conductivity. There were therefore conflicting models that at very low temperatures metals might be either very good conductors or insulators. Experiments were therefore needed, and Kamerlingh Onnes found that mercury follows the trend for the former model, but at 4.2 K the electrical resistance fell precipitously to zero. He received the Nobel prize for this discovery. This loss of resistance occurs in most metals and can be complete. The solenoids used to generate the magnetic fields used for Magnetic Resonance Imaging (MRI) systems are made with superconducting wire held close to 4.2 K, and are set up with circulating electrical currents that persist for months or years without any reduction (so long as the wires are kept cold).

Superconductivity remained phenomenology for half a century. The theory that captures the essence of its cause was produced by Bardeen, Cooper and Schrieffer in 1957, for which the second Nobel prize associated with superconductivity was awarded. They proposed that electrons can pair up with one another at low temperatures. They showed how this could happen if they can both distort the local positions of atoms in the metal (through very much the same mechanism that causes single electrons to be scattered by the atoms at high temperatures). The significance of the pairing of the electrons is that this switches them from obeying the rules of quantum mechanics for Fermi particles, or fermions, to those for Bose particles or bosons. Whereas only one fermion can occupy a quantum state, bosons are not constrained, so that the superconducting electron pairs all fall into a very low kinetic energy state and travel around as a coherent wave that is not easily disturbed.

Materials technology progressed slowly too. Higher superconducting temperatures were found among many metals and alloys, but progress was modest, and only alloys with the A15 crystal structure such as Nb_3Sn could approach the boiling temperature of hydrogen. Indeed, by the early 1980s the general view was that higher superconducting transition temperatures would never be found, and an explanation had been advanced – if the interactions between electrons and the lattice of atoms needed for superconductivity were too strong then it would destabilize that crystalline structure of the metals and cause a different crystalline structure to form. Enthusiasm to unify and simplify runs the risk that a pattern of phenomena is mistaken for a law of science. As we now know, such was the case here.

TECHNOLOGY FROM CHEMISTRY: CUPRATE HIGH TEMPERATURE SUPERCONDUCTORS

The community that searched for better superconductors in the 1970s and 1980s restricted its range to materials that were similar to the then known superconductors, and, for the most part not being chemists, they kept the chemical composition relatively simple. There had been a number of unsubstantiated reports that very different materials classes might superconduct. There were, for example, reports from Russia that cuprous oxide showed very high conductivity at high hydrostatic pressure, but this was not confirmed elsewhere and probably was the result of disproportionation into cupric oxide and metallic copper. However, Bednorz and Müller at the IBM Laboratory in Zurich put out a paper in 1986 claiming that barium-doped lanthanum cuprate appeared to show superconductivity at temperatures near 30 K (Bednorz and Müller 1986). This paper was picked up in Japan and when the results were reproduced there, this generated a huge stampede as many hundreds of scientists threw themselves into the charge. This class of materials had been relatively well studied within a different community, of solid-state chemists, and there are reports from France as far back as 1982 showing metallic behaviour down to the temperature of liquid nitrogen, 77 K, the limit of their measurements (Nguyen, Studer and Raveau 1983). It was, of course, Bednorz and Muller who won the third Nobel prize for superconductivity, but for the many hundreds who joined in the rewards were far slimmer.

Rule 2 Avoid crowds

Working in a crowded field can generate plenty of adrenaline, but is not often a wise strategic choice. Most of the easy pickings have usually been taken before you have started, and there are too many groups around the world who are better practitioners than devisers of new projects.

In 1987 the abandonment of the usual professional values in the field of so-called 'high temperature superconductivity' came close to the tulipmania of seventeenth-century Netherlands as the frenetic pursuit of superconductors with higher and higher transition temperatures gathered pace. The big boys in the USA were the groups in the corporate research laboratories, particularly Bell Laboratories at Murray Hill in New Jersey, and they threw their industrial might into play. The usual professional standards seemed to slip in the rush to claim precedence. The delay between submission of papers to learned journals and their appearance in print fell close to the point where independent and thoughtful refereeing was not possible. The premier journal for the field was *Physical Review Letters*, and in saner times the standards set by referees usually stretches publication out to at least six months from submission. However, the Bell Labs group had their first paper published on 26 January 1987, less than a month after submission on 29 December 1986, even though this paper did little more than confirm what Bednorz and Muller had already published (Cava *et al.* 1987).

One very significant advance was reported by the group of Chu at the University of Houston in March 1987. They had found a new family of cuprate materials with superconducting transition temperatures above the boiling temperature of liquid nitrogen, 77 K. Liquid nitrogen is cheap, and is a very practical refrigerant, so getting past 77 K was an important milestone. There is an oft-repeated story – more or less confirmed in the account of this 'fools' gold rush' by Hazen (1988) – that captures the moment. Chu *et al.* were, not unreasonably, very concerned that their magic formula might be tested in the laboratories of the referees selected by *Physical Review Letters*, and, of course, these same referees might at the same time find reason to delay acceptance of the paper they were refereeing. Chu *et al.* had found a material comprised of yttrium, barium, copper and oxygen, but it is said that the manuscript submitted to the journal showed a rare-earth metal, ytterbium, in place of yttrium. Presumably Chu *et al.* had had the sense to confirm that ytterbium does not in fact work too. The story then goes that this 'typographical error' was corrected only at the very last minute, just before the paper (Wu *et al.* 1987) was published!

This is not a good environment to work in, and particularly so if you have a whole career ahead of you. Citation statistics show very clearly that the only papers that really stand head and shoulders above the rest are those that are first. The first paper from Bednorz and Müller (1986) has now (February 2008) been cited more than 7,300 times in other scientific journal publications. This is followed by the paper from Chu (Wu *et al.* 1987) at around 4,400 citations. The rest are way behind, somewhere in the noise. Why would you want to work in a field where more than 7,000 learned scientific papers draw on one discovery?

As a footnote, one can record that 20 years on, the practical difficulties in the engineering and processing of high temperature superconductors have severely limited their application. Instead, standard superconducting metallic alloys of niobium and titanium are used as the superconducting wires in MRI superconducting solenoids. The mechanisms for superconductivity still elude a universally accepted model, though this is an important scientific question.

> Rule 3   Tread warily with theory: it usually explains things after they have been discovered

This is tricky territory, but unless you are as brilliant as Paul Dirac or Brian Josephson, you are unlikely to predict something really new from your theoretical contemplations and modelling. Entirely correctly, we celebrate those very rare instances where deep insight generates discovery. Paul Dirac's solution of the relativistic Schrödinger equation for the electron produced solutions in which the mass of the electron could be either positive or negative, and rather than throw away the latter option, Dirac recognized that mass could be negative. The positron antimatter companion to the electron has duly joined the bestiary of fundamental subatomic particles. Brian Josephson considered what might happen if the superconducting electron pair could simultaneously tunnel across a non-superconducting barrier between two superconductors and predicted that the current would oscillate in proportion to the voltage across the junction. No experimental scientist had expected that this could happen, but experiments confirmed this is so, and indeed this now provides the standard for measurement of voltage.

These discoveries in the field of superconductivity have all happened unexpectedly in the laboratory because the right chance experiment was done. This is much the more frequent route to discovery. Theory has later made a major contribution to our understanding, but did not predict the phenomena.

Rule 4 Don't read the literature (or, suspend belief/disbelief if you do)

I know this is a shocking suggestion, but my premise is very simple. There is so much material out there in the literature that firstly, you would never have time to read it all. Secondly, if you did, you would probably convince yourself that everything had been done already. Thirdly, you would almost certainly find reasons why your own ideas would not work. The scientific literature is not a digest of what is generally considered to be correct, but merely the accumulation of what has got past the journal referees. Very little of what is published turns out to be sufficiently relevant to be cited by other authors, much of it is unimportant in-fill, some of it is misleading and, too frequently, much of it is simply wrong. As a community we do not stop and clean things up – we simply move on.

The rate of increase in the volume of published material would have been unsustainable if it had been available only as printed pages.

The Physical Review – 1960   *The Physical Review* – 2005

FIGURE 15 Bound copies of the *Physical Review* in the Rayleigh Library in the Cavendish Laboratory for 1960 and for 2005 (copyright R. H. Friend).

Figure 15 shows the stacked volumes of the *Physical Review* (the journal of the American Physical Society) for 1960 and for 2005. The six bound volumes from 1960, totalling around 6,000 pages, are clearly well read and well thumbed. It was just about possible then to be aware of everything published in physics that year. By 2005 we have lost control – the 78 bound volumes total around 80,000 pages – far too much to even skim. These volumes clearly have never been opened – I suspect I was the first person to take them off the shelves when I set them up to photograph. We now find our way through this jungle with the aid of electronic databases and read the occasional paper on line.

In my own field, we have regularly been assured that what we are trying to do will not work because literature in similar fields proves that it cannot. So far this advice has been wrong on all occasions and we have been able to take our polymer semiconductors far further than the sceptics had told us we could go. Sometimes the base for these concerns has been wholly reasonable. There was a lot of concern in the mid 1990s that the polymer semiconductors we were using to make our light-emitting diodes could not emit light efficiently. The argument was that though an isolated polymer chain might fluoresce efficiently, once packed together to form a solid assembly the interactions between adjacent polymer chains would cause the electronic excitation on the polymer chain to be unable to emit a photon. There was a stream of very plausible papers from Bell Laboratories that apparently demonstrated this was so, and that pronounced that therefore lasers could not be produced from these materials (Yan *et al.* 1994). We duly demonstrated that lasers are easily made with these materials (Tessler, Denton and Friend 1996). The reconciliation of these two positions came later; it turns out that the electronic excitation that later produces a photon is very spread out along the chain of the polymer, and this switches off the quenching process that the group at Bell Laboratories had been concerned about. I am not sure why we decided to persevere – I think it was probably a hunch that the experiment was worth doing, just in case.

Rule 5   Do not underestimate the power of engineering

Scientists are not in general very good at predicting the course of engineering and technology. We are often not well placed to understand what the limitations to the performance of our nascent technologies may be. It is wise therefore not to be early to dismiss the application of your discoveries because they do not seem to perform well enough or to last for long enough. There are many documented examples where first exemplifications were short-lived and underperforming, but which later provide very reliable and widely used devices. Kressel provides an account of the first laser diodes made with III-V semiconductors that were notoriously prone to failure but are now used in their millions in CD and DVD players (Kressel 2007). Many thousands of hours of materials engineering sorted out the reasons for early failure, which were mostly extrinsic defects, and performance is now outstanding. The optical fibres used to transmit information across oceans show extraordinarily low attenuation, well beyond the expectations we had when optical fibres were first developed in the 1970s. This has been achieved by sustained and brilliant engineering.

Our work with polymer semiconductors has followed at least part of this pathway. Our first devices were not very long-lived, but materials and process engineering at Cambridge Display Technology has lifted lifetimes from a few hours in our first devices to (projected) lifetimes well beyond 100,000 hours (about 10 years continuous operation). Our first transistors in 1988 were neither well-performing nor long-lived, but we can now make transistors with improved polymers that work reliably even without encapsulation to keep out air. We have also developed new ways to manufacture these transistors (Sirringhaus 2000), and are exploiting these through Plastic Logic Ltd, which was spun out from the University in 2000. Plastic Logic makes arrays of plastic transistors directly on plastic substrates that can be used to drive an electrophoretic display foil from E-ink to produce a flexible electronic paper display, as shown in Figure 16.

Rule 6 Never become dependent on a single source of research funding

If you have taken the decision to head off the beaten track, you will face a major challenge. Research costs money and you will have to find this from a grant-giving body. When you seek funding for a high-risk project in an area in which you are not already known to be expert, you may naïvely consider that this is not for industrial support, but instead that you should seek funding from governmental funding agencies (in the UK the Research Councils). Beware! Research Councils take decisions at committees of your peers. When there are ten or more committee members, outlier projects are very rarely funded. Too often the support ends up being distributed around the community to preserve a state of more-or-less equal contentment or discontentment. I think this is not malice, incompetence or self-interest, but just the functioning of the dynamics of a group of this size. I was very lucky to get support for our speculative research on polymers from industry. In industry, decisions to offer support are generally taken by one person, and this changes the outcome. David Bott at British Petroleum provided me with a lot of support in the early days, and it was only later when our results were sufficiently robust that we forced our way through the peer review system with the Research Council, who have since supported us very well.

It is not wise to be dependent on just one funding organization, even though they may be long-term and supportive, you will probably adjust what you do in order to stay in line with what they think you should be doing. Even if you are well looked after by your main provider of support,

FIGURE 16 Early stage demonstration of a flexible electronic paper display formed with an active matrix backplane of plastic transistors laminated with an electronic display foil (copyright Plastic Logic Ltd).

it is wise to get just a part of your funding from elsewhere, so that this allows you to try out something off your projected path.

Conclusion

I have intended to reassure the young physics researcher (and, perhaps, researchers more generally) that discovery can be just around the corner, as it always has been. I hope I have not, along the way, raised too many new concerns. For those that are prepared to take an independent path the prospects for serendipitous discovery are just as great as they were in the past.

References

Bednorz, J. G. and K. A. Müller (1986) 'Possible high tc super-conductivity in the Ba-La-Cu-O system', *Zeitschrift für Physik B* 64, 189.

Burroughes, J. H., D. D. C. Bradley, A. R. Brown, *et al.* (1990) 'Light-emitting diodes based on conjugated polymers', *Nature* 347, 539.

Burroughes, J. H., C. A. Jones and R. H. Friend (1988) 'New semiconductor device physics in polymer diodes and transistors', *Nature* 335, 137.

Cava, R. J., R. B. van Dover, B. Batlogg and E. A. Rietman (1987) 'Bulk superconductivity at 36K in La1.8Sr0.2CuO4', *Physical Review Letters* 58, 408.

Hazen, R. M. (1988) *The Breakthrough*. New York: Summit Books.

Kressel, H. (2007) *Competing for the Future: How Digital Innovations Are Changing the World*. Cambridge: Cambridge University Press.

Nguyen, N., F. Studer and B. Raveau (1983) 'Oxydes ternaires de cuivre à valence mixte de type K_2NiF_4 deficitaires en oxygène: évolution progressive d'un état semi-conducteur vers un état semi-métallique des oxydes La_2-xSr$_x$CuO$_{4-x}$/2 + d', *Journal of Physics and Chemistry of Solids* 44, 389.

Sirringhaus, H., T. Kawase, R. H. Friend, *et al.* (2000) 'High-resolution inkjet printing of all-polymer transistor circuits', *Science* 290, 2123.

Tessler, N., G. J. Denton and R. H. Friend (1996) 'Lasing from conjugated-polymer microcavities', *Nature* 382, 695.

Wu, M. K., J. R. Ashburn, C. J. Torng, *et al.* (1987) 'Superconductivity at 93K in a new mixed phase Y-Ba-Cu-O compound system', *Physical Review Letters* 58, 908.

Yan, M., L. J. Rothberg, F. Papadimitrakopoulos, M. E. Galvin and T. M. Miller (1994) 'Spatially indirect excitons as the primary photoexcitations in conjugated polymers', *Physical Review Letters* 72, 1104.

7 Liberalism and uncertainty

OLIVER LETWIN

I ought to begin with a confession. I am a long-term adherent of what E. H. Carr called 'the Cleopatra's nose theory of history'. I am fully persuaded that the shape of Cleopatra's nose had an effect on Mark Antony; and that their relationship had an effect on history.

Certainly, there is such a thing as the movement of ideas. And I wouldn't want to deny, either, the fundamental importance of institutional structures or of economic realities. But we shouldn't underestimate the role of accident when it comes to determining what actually comes to pass in our world.

Whether the accidents are happy or otherwise is, of course, another question. Who is to know whether the beauty of Cleopatra's nose in the eyes of Mark Antony was a happy or unhappy coincidence? It depends on your perspective. What was good for Cleopatra was not necessarily good for her subjects.

Indeed, I take the view that – even from a given perspective – the quality of accident as chance or as mischance is itself accidental. It isn't until long after the event, and after many other occurrences, that one really knows whether the event itself was a happy or an unhappy thing. Chou En-lai was perhaps exaggerating but he was nevertheless on the right lines when he said, upon being asked for his assessment of the French Revolution, that it was too early to tell.

Now, if all this is true of history, then it must be true also of politics, which is, after all, history in the making. The great sweep of politics is the great sweep of history – the movement of ideas, the institutional structures, the economic realities. But the events in political life that

Serendipity, edited by Mark de Rond and Iain Morley.
Published by Cambridge University Press. © Darwin College 2010.

make and shape the specific present are hugely a matter of happy or unhappy coincidence. Every politician of every caste of mind will tell you that the same thing done or said, or omitted or left unsaid, at one moment will be ignored and unimportant; at another, will become a crux because of its coincidence with other chance occurrences. And these cruxes can be of lasting importance because they can lead to shifts in power that have real and lasting effects on ideas, on structures and on economies.

But I do not wish here to mount a defence of Cleopatra's nose in the face of the onslaught from the theoreticians – the Hegelians, the Marxists, the Structuralists and the other 'ians' and 'ists' who expend so much intellect and passion in explaining to us all why the accidents, after all, are either not really accidents or are just accidents, swept along in the inevitable tide of historical and political certainty. I have a dark suspicion that, however many times one finds an accident which appears to have changed the course of history or politics, our friendly theoreticians will find an explanation of why the deeper dialectic made the outcome inevitable, regardless of whether that accident or some other had occurred. And I do not have any appetite for that ceaseless argument.

I want, instead, to make a different sort of argument about the relationship between politics and the phenomenon of discovery by happy accident that Horace Walpole first called by the name of this series of essays. I want to argue that the importance or lack of importance we attach to uncertainty is a fundamental determinant of our political outlook. More specifically, I want to argue that liberalism is founded upon emphasizing the role of uncertainty in politics, because liberalism depends upon attending to citizen-reaction rather than merely to government-action.

It is a strange feature of modern political discourse that we hear a great deal more about government-action than about citizen-reaction. In a totalitarian state, this would be natural. The purpose of government in a totalitarian state is to command outcomes and to use an apparatus of terror to ensure that these outcomes occur. In such a system, government-action is what counts. Citizen-reaction can be discounted. But, for a liberal – whether a liberal Conservative such as myself, or any other sort of liberal-minded politician – things are very different. A liberal starts from the proposition that government is, or at least ought to be, governing citizens who are free to choose.

For a liberal, there cannot be any automatic assumption that government-action will lead to a given outcome. The liberal has to ask, instead, what will be the citizen-reaction to any government-action? And for a liberal, any answer to that question must always include a considerable degree of uncertainty, since there cannot be certainty where events depend on free choice.

Of course, there are limits to liberalism – and limits to freedom. A liberal is not an anarchist. A liberal can accept what Oakeshott called 'adverbial constraints' on the freedom to choose. Rules of the 'whatever you do, and however you do it, don't do this' variety are part of a liberal democracy. 'Whatever you do, don't murder others as the way of achieving it.' 'However you get there, don't get there by driving at 100 mph on the wrong side of the road.'

But the laws that establish these adverbial constraints on action – though rightly much debated in a liberal democracy – actually constitute only a tiny fraction of the activity of the modern state. Most government-action is far more specific and far more ephemeral.

The setting of interest rates by the Monetary Policy Committee of the Bank of England is, in a slightly extended sense, a government-action. But it is not a law establishing an Oakeshottian adverbial constraint. It leaves the citizen free to choose how to respond. No one will be put in prison if they decide to go on spending and borrowing despite a rise in interest rates, or if they decide not to spend or borrow despite a fall in interest rates. The setting of interest rates is, in other words, a government-action which depends for its effect on the nature of the citizen-reaction that it provokes. The government-action in itself achieves nothing. All that it does – all that it *can* do – is done through the reaction of citizens who are free to choose.

Now, I argue that engendering the desired citizen-reaction in this case is bound to be, from the point of view of government, a matter of uncertainty. The nature of the citizen-reaction will depend upon coincidences that government can neither control nor accurately predict.

'Hold on a moment,' I hear the economists complain. 'Don't we very well know that reduced interest rates lead to increased borrowing, and that increased interest rates lead to reduced borrowing?' Well, up to a point, Lord Copper. Directionally, we do. But – as the Bank of Japan discovered over a long and painful period – if the reduction in interest rates coincides with sufficient lack of confidence on the part of citizens who are free to choose, they may freely choose to pay no attention whatsoever to shifts of interest rates by which they would have been greatly influenced under other circumstances.

And this is typical of the way in which government-action influences citizen-reaction. Day by day, week by week, we witness the spectacle of governments pulling levers that are found to have nothing, or unexpected items, at the other end.

An effort is made to assist single parents. The reaction, clearly unanticipated by government, is that people who were previously living together reorganize their affairs to 'live together apart' – living apart for the purposes of government, but together for other purposes. An attempt is made to encourage emerging renewable technologies in power generation. The reaction, clearly unanticipated by government, is that profits are accumulated by the promotion of mature onshore-wind technologies – leaving the emerging technologies as emerging as before.

There is no end to the ability of government to generate unintended consequences when it acts in ways which focus on government-action and which ignore or underrate the potential for unexpected citizen-reaction. My argument today is that one of the deepest divisions in political life is between the two possible responses to this fact of indeterminacy in politics.

Illiberal politics is founded upon hatred of indeterminacy. It seeks to eliminate uncertainty by ensuring that government-action is translated directly into determinate outcome. And that, of course, can be achieved only by robbing the citizen of the power to choose. Illiberal politics therefore moves swiftly from the proposition that 'the government has done X' to the proposition that 'the citizen must do Y'. Every government action takes on the character of a command. Illiberal government becomes a command-system in which government seeks to determine events with certainty.

The hallmark of liberal politics, by contrast, is an acceptance of uncertainty, an acceptance that government-action will typically become effective only through the mediation of uncertain citizen-reaction. In liberal politics, government accepts that uncertainty is the necessary companion of the freedom of the citizen to choose. The art of liberal politics becomes not the mechanical achievement of outcomes by direct government-action but the exercise of judgement about the citizen-reaction that is likely to be provoked by government-action.

Before I go on to describe what consequences this acceptance of uncertainty has for the nature of liberal-minded politics, I want to point out how dangerously unfamiliar this terrain has become to us over the last century or so.

Let's try a little thought-experiment. How surprised would you be to switch on your radio or to look at your online news bulletin in the morning and hear or read that the government was doing such-and-such? I speculate that, unless the action by government were in itself unusual, the answer is 'not very'. To hear that government is acting is, in itself, unsurprising to us. We expect governments to act. Indeed, it would be surprising to hear that government was being purposefully *in*active.

Now imagine, by contrast, a morning when the radio or the e-bulletin announced that government was predicting that the citizen-reaction to its latest move would be such-and-such. Would that surprise you? I speculate that it would. I speculate that you cannot recall a recent occasion on which some representative of government in whatever part of the world announced that they were doing X because they hoped that it would lead people to react by doing Y. It sounds, to the modern ear, so weedy, doesn't it? We seem to want our governments to be more manly than that! Problem. Government-action. Solution. That's the ticket. Not merely an earnest hope that 'if X, then likely Y'.

In short, our political discourse – the language in which both politicians and commentators speak and are expected to speak – in modern liberal democratic politics is itself dangerously illiberal. It unconsciously promotes the idea that government-action has the necessary form of a command to be enforced, rather than often taking the form of activity whose effects are mediated by the reactions of free citizens. So part of my purpose is to make a plea that we should begin to alter our political language.

We should begin explicitly to recognize that, in a liberal society, citizen-reaction is as important as government-action, and that uncertainty is part of the fabric of a politics that is truly liberal.

I want next to address those central propositions about liberal-minded politics today which flow from the argument I have made so far. First, I want to persuade you that the acceptance of uncertainty due to citizen-reaction in politics has a profound consequence for the way that those of us who are professional politicians in a liberal democracy ought to conceive of what we are doing. Second, I want to persuade you that there is a particular historical context within which we are operating, which also has profound consequences for the way in which we ought to conceive of what we are doing. And third, I want to persuade you that the context within which we are now operating gives uncertainty an even more central role in liberal politics today than it has had in the past.

First, any well-intentioned liberal-minded politician who is aiming at social goods and who accepts that citizen-reaction has to be taken seriously must accept two obvious entailments. First, he must accept that the consequences of government-action can be predicted (even to the extent of assessing *likely* citizen-reactions) only if such assessments are *holistic*: we can tell how citizens are likely to react only if we have a good grip on all the relevant circumstances that affect their decisions. Second, the liberal-minded politician must accept that government-action will make a given set of citizen-reactions likely only if the frameworks established by government make those reactions rational for citizens in the light of all the relevant circumstances.

These obvious entailments lead to a particular view of what a well-intentioned politician who is seeking social goods and who is committed to liberalism should conceive himself to be doing. Namely, he should conceive himself to be in the business of attempting to establish frameworks within which, taking all relevant circumstances into account, it becomes rational and hence likely that citizens will react in ways that are socially beneficial.

For the liberal, this conception of frameworks that 'tilt' rational choice towards socially responsible ends is fundamental. There is all the difference in the world between the proposition that 'the politician believes it to be in the interest of society at large that you should do X, and he will therefore make it unlawful for you to do other than X', and the proposition that 'the politician believes it to be in the interest of society at large that you should do X, and he will therefore seek to establish frameworks within which it will be rational for you to act responsibly and to do X'.

In the first case, where X is commanded or prohibited by law, the politician needs to establish a precise definition of X, capable of precise legal enforcement, and he needs to establish a process of effective enforcement almost inevitably involving extension of state power. Beyond this, the politician needs to be sure that it will *always* be socially beneficial for the citizen to comply with what the law specifies – since statute law is a blunt instrument which allows no exceptions, and it would be counterproductive to compel a citizen to do X if, for that citizen, given all the circumstances, it was socially irresponsible to do X.

In the second case, by contrast, where the action held to be leading to a social good is made rational for the citizen by the creation of a framework of incentives, the politician does not need to establish precise definitions of the action, since there is no question of legal enforcement. For the same reason, the politician in this case does not need to establish a process of effective enforcement and hence does not need to extend state power. And the politician does not need to be sure that it will always be beneficial for the citizen to do X, since the framework is only a framework of incentives and leaves the citizen free to balance the general incentives provided by that framework to do X, against other reasons for acting in a different way on this particular occasion.

In short, a politics founded on frameworks that tilt rational citizen-choice towards social responsibility is intrinsically more liberal than a politics founded on legal command and legal inhibition. Politicians who conceive themselves as being involved principally *not* in passing laws to compel or prohibit given actions, but in constructing frameworks which make it rational for citizens to react in socially responsible ways, are intrinsically more liberal than politicians whose sole focus is on command and prohibition.

It is important to note that this account of liberalism and of its relationship to citizen-reaction locates liberalism in the *method* of conducting politics rather than in the substantive aims of a particular politician or of a particular political party at any given time. Liberal-minded politicians of differing persuasions can disagree at any given time about the social benefits that it is most important for the framework of incentive to bring about. But it is equally important to recognize that this scope for disagreement about social priorities between truly liberal-minded politicians of differing persuasions is not unlimited. The liberal method sets limits on the range of substantive aims because the liberal method is essentially democratic.

If the main activity of the liberal politician is conceived as the setting of frameworks within which it is rational to expect certain likely citizen-reactions, then it becomes incoherent for the liberal-minded politician to adopt aims which are fundamentally at odds with the deepest feelings of the citizen-body, since it is inconceivable that frameworks of incentives could be constructed that would make it rational for free citizens to choose to do what conflicts with their deepest feelings.

In other words, liberalism – if conceived in terms of encouraging likely citizen-reactions – automatically limits itself to aims which are congruent with the deepest feelings of the citizen-body, and hence automatically prevents itself from imposing upon the citizen-body aims which are fundamentally antipathetic. At the same time, a politics conceived principally in terms of encouraging likely reactions, rather than imposing certain outcomes, automatically allows for eccentricity. When a framework of incentives is established, those citizens who have sufficiently strong dispositions to act in ways other than those encouraged by the incentives will do so. This, indeed, is why – in relation to massively anti-social activity – the liberal accepts the need for legal compulsion and legal prohibition. But, where a *general* result is judged sufficient to bring about a social good, and a framework of incentives is therefore preferred to legal compulsion or prohibition, room is left for the eccentric to ignore the incentives provided by the framework. This conscious acceptance that the likely normal citizen-reaction will not necessarily be the universal citizen-reaction to government-action is one of the hallmarks of a liberal attitude to politics. Liberalism without a place for eccentricity is not true liberalism.

I am conscious that this account of liberalism – in terms of an attitude to government – contrasts with standard accounts that dwell on respect for individual and group rights. There is, of course, no incompatibility between these two different aspects of liberal-minded politics. It is an important – indeed, a defining – characteristic of liberal-minded politics of all persuasions that it establishes and respects individual and minority group rights. Alan Ryan is undoubtedly right to argue that one of the deepest tensions within liberal political theory is the tension between respect for individual rights and respect for minority group rights where these come into conflict with one another.

But, whilst respect for individual and group rights is certainly a necessary condition for liberal politics, I argue that it is by no means a sufficient description. A regime may be committed to respect for individual and group rights and yet be thoroughly illiberal. Three obvious examples spring to mind: ID cards, universal conscription and very high levels of taxation. None of these conflicts with basic human or natural rights as such rights are generally understood. Forcing people to carry ID cards, operating a system of military conscription and levying very high taxes are all permitted under the European Convention on Human Rights. Moreover, although I happen to believe that each of these three policies is inappropriate in today's Britain, each might be defended by someone of a liberal disposition as necessary at some time – for example, during the Second World War.

But each of these policies – whether justified or unjustified at a given time in a given place – is clearly and fundamentally illiberal, in the sense that each clearly restricts the freedom of the citizen, and each tends to establish a relationship of command between state and citizen. You can defend ID cards, or conscription, or very high levels of taxation on various grounds at certain crises – but you cannot plausibly defend them on the grounds that they are liberal measures. And this despite the fact that none of them conflicts with basic human rights. We accordingly need a description of liberalism which goes beyond merely respecting such rights.

What we need is a description of liberalism which – unlike the minimalist condition of respecting basic human rights – adequately captures the liberalism of liberal measures and adequately captures the illiberalism of illiberal measures, without falling into the trap of confusing liberalism with anarchism. My argument today is that such a description of liberalism can be given only when one recognizes that a defining characteristic of liberal-minded politics is the preference, wherever possible, for frameworks that make given citizen-reactions more likely, rather than for compulsion and prohibitions that aim to produce certainty.

In modern politics where we all accept the role of the state in promoting socially beneficial results, the true road to serfdom is the road from framework of incentives to universal command, and the true road to freedom is the road from universal command to framework of incentives. In other words, Hayek was right to identify the command-economy as a fundamentally illiberal proposition but wrong to suggest that the distinction between command and framework in management of the economy was any more fundamental than the distinction between command and framework in the social (as opposed to economic) sphere. Frameworks of incentives that allow for citizen-reaction and for eccentricity are essentially liberal; commands and prohibitions – however Oakeshottian, however respectful of basic human rights, and however justified – are essentially illiberal.

It has recently become particularly important to enlarge the description of liberalism to extend beyond mere respect for rights and to include the acceptance by the state of uncertainty and eccentricity. This is because we have recently entered, or are at least on the threshold of, a new post-bureaucratic age in politics. Let me explain what I mean by this assertion. Time was – time out of mind ago – when our predecessors in Britain and the rest of Europe lived in a pre-bureaucratic age. In that pre-bureaucratic age, power was decentralized – not because anyone had decentralized it but because it was impossible for anyone to centralize it. Poor communications between the centre and the periphery, combined (*pace* the Domesday Book) with a low level of information about the periphery at the centre, made it well-nigh impossible for the centre to micro-manage the periphery. Kings struggled mightily, but largely unsuccessfully, to establish any significant degree of control over what was done locally.

What followed, in early modern and modern times, was a bureaucratic age. The improvement of communications and the development of an increasing bureaucracy at the centre (armed with ledgers, card indices and, latterly, computers) made it increasingly possible for the centre to find out about, to analyse and to micro-manage the periphery. As Weber and others pointed out, the level of information available at the centre made it (or at least appeared to make it) rational for many decisions to be made centrally. The bureaucracy had the means to be better informed about the state of flood defences or schooling in Wotton-under-Edge than the inhabitants of Wotton-under-Edge themselves, and a rational case could therefore be made for micro-management of those affairs by the bureaucracy.

We have now entered, or are at least now entering, a new era – a post-bureaucratic age, in which the bureaucracy is losing its privileged access to information. Open networks make as much difference to the relationship between citizen and bureaucrat as the spread of literacy and the invention of printing once made to the relationship between the Church-hierarchy and the believer. Just as the availability of printed bibles, once translated into the vernacular, enabled literate believers to challenge accepted interpretation of the text, so the citizen, armed with a PC and broadband, is now able to gather and analyse information drawn from sources around the world, and is hence able to challenge what was previously the unchallengeable expertise of the bureaucracy.

Why does the dawning of the post-bureaucratic age give citizen-reaction a new place in politics? Because the coming of open networks, and the levelling effect they have on what was once the privileged access of bureaucracy to information, removes a great part of the rationale for centralized command and compulsion. In an age when the bureaucrat was able to access information which the citizen was in no position to obtain, it could be argued that the bureaucracy was so much better placed than the citizen to determine beneficial outcomes as to justify the bureaucracy imposing those beneficial outcomes through an array of compulsions and prohibitions. With the advent of open networks and of equal access to information, the position changes. The argument for the superior rationality of the bureaucracy, and hence the argument for the bureaucracy to bring about socially beneficial results through compulsion and prohibition, becomes weaker.

There remain, of course, differences between self-interest and the wider interests of society at large. Open networks do not change human nature. It remains the case that a great purpose of government is to bring about socially beneficial results where short-term self-interest will otherwise lead to socially irresponsible results. But, in an open network society, it becomes much easier to operate through liberal frameworks of incentives.

Once the network-enabled citizen is well informed about comparative outcomes, government can create frameworks that give the citizen the means and incentive to choose whichever of the available socially responsible options – in healthcare, in education, in decentralized energy – will best meet that citizen's desires and expectations. In this way, government comes to rely not on bureaucratically engineered certainties but on the general effects of incentive and opportunity to achieve socially beneficial goals. And this manner of governing – accepting that the desired results will be achieved in general but cannot be individually ensured with certainty in advance – is essentially liberal because it respects not just individual rights but also the eccentricity that inevitably accompanies the grant to individuals of power and opportunity in their lives.

In the end, after all the theorizing, there are really only two attitudes to governing adopted by people of goodwill: benevolent authoritarianism and benevolent liberalism. And, of course, there is something of each of these dispositions in all forms of well-intentioned governance. Even the most authoritarian of benevolent authoritarians has some liberal hesitations; and even the most liberal of benevolent liberals recognizes the need for some authoritarian compulsions and prohibitions. But there remains a fundamental divide between the two attitudes.

The benevolent authoritarian is at root a pessimist. He sees the natural life of the citizen-body as consisting of, at best, a random set of occurrences with little social value and, at worst, a destructive chaos.

The benevolent liberal is, by contrast, an optimist. He sees the natural life of the citizen-body as consisting of a set of outcomes which will be discovered to have social value.

The benevolent authoritarian derives from his pessimism a desire to compel and prohibit – to rescue by those means social value from social chaos. He sees himself as a chess player who is moving citizens around a chessboard.

The benevolent liberal, by contrast, derives from his optimism a respect for the autonomy of the citizen – and seeks to enhance the social value of those citizens' autonomous choices by creating frameworks of incentives within which it becomes more likely that those choices will be socially beneficial. Instead of seeing himself as a chess player, the benevolent liberal sees himself as an impresario, bringing together a great festival out of a thousand different shows. An optimistic faith in the outcome of the uncertainties of a free society is not, in short, an incidental feature of the liberal-minded attitude to governing: it is the hallmark of such an attitude.

We should feel privileged to be living at a time when the open networks of a post-bureaucratic age are increasingly justifying that liberal-minded optimism – increasingly enabling the citizen-body to bring about socially valuable results within liberal frameworks of incentives and opportunity.

8 The unanticipated pleasures of the writing life

SIMON WINCHESTER

As I speak*, I have just returned from Sri Lanka, the conceptual birthplace of Serendipity – and something serendipitous did indeed happen there. It is rather a sweet story, one that I will return to in concluding this essay. This contribution is a rather more personal one than some, as I want to explain how my career has largely been marked by serendipitous occurrences, unexpected delights that have channelled me this way and that. I'm going to begin by telling you of something that occurred maybe six or seven years ago and, though it didn't have anything specific to do with my career, stands as an indication of the kind of unexpected delight that seems to have peppered my life over the years.

I was coming back from the Antarctic on a Russian icebreaker, which was going on an extremely long journey from the Antarctic Peninsula, wallowing its way up the Atlantic Ocean to Murmansk. It was a long and boring journey and the vessel was not particularly attractive or comfortable. We were lumbering along at eight or ten knots and so the journey was going to take an interminable time and I really wanted to get back home to New York where I live.

We were somewhere near the Equator off West Africa. I was on the bridge one day looking at the charts and I realized that we weren't terribly far away from Ascension Island, which I'd been to once or twice before. And I remembered that there was a weekly Royal Air Force flight between Brize Norton in Oxfordshire, Ascension and the Falkland Islands. I figured that possibly I could get permission, and providing the

* This is a word-for-word transcription of the lecture given by Mr Winchester, which was made *ad libitum*.

Serendipity, edited by Mark de Rond and Iain Morley.
Published by Cambridge University Press. © Darwin College 2010.

123

captain didn't mind nudging the boat a little bit to starboard to drop me off at Ascension, and could catch the RAF plane north.

So a couple of radio telephone calls were made to the Administrator of Ascension Island – which is, for anyone thinking of going into the diplomatic service, not a post exactly at the cutting edge of British diplomacy. He basically said yes to both of my requests. I was to be allowed to come onto the island, and the RAF agreed that I could fly back to Brize Norton with them. The next northbound aircraft would be departing in four days' time or so.

So the captain steered the ship such that Ascension came into view on the starboard beam, whereupon he stood off about a mile, hove to and lowered a boat for me. You can fly to Ascension quite easily, but landing by ship is extremely difficult. Moreover, there are these steps called the Tudor Steps which are covered with seaweed and extremely slippery, and the Atlantic rollers that wash onto them are very, very dangerous. A majestically sized Russian seaman rowed me over to them and essentially threw me onto these steps. There is a worn-out hemp rope you catch onto – it's terrifying – then he threw my rucksack onto land, and I hauled myself up through the slime and he rowed away as fast as he could, going back to his ship and his vodka and his evening's amusements.

So I was hauling myself soaked and sort of embarrassed and humiliated up these steps and eventually breasted the skyline. Normally when you stay on Ascension, if you're not a guest of the Air Force, which I wasn't, you stay in an old leprosy hospital, which isn't a particularly comfortable billet. That's what I imagined would happen. But on this day standing at the top of the steps, beaming, was this pink-faced, curly-haired man with a dog-collar on – by which I mean a priest's collar – and he said 'Hello, my name is Nigel', or something like that. 'I'm the vicar here and I gather you're coming to stay for a few days. My wife Angela and I would be simply thrilled if you'd come and stay at the vicarage.' Who knew there was a vicarage on Ascension Island? So I stayed with them and it was absolutely ideal, they were nice, bright, kind, lovely people.

Before long, the day of my departure arrived. Basically the southbound plane had already been through – one saw it land, refuel and then take off for the South Atlantic to go down to the Falkland Islands – and then it was due to arrive back at about 2 o'clock in the morning on this

Thursday, and would land at Brize Norton at about six in the morning. I had reservations on a flight back to New York from Heathrow at about one in the afternoon. It all looked as if it was going to work like clockwork.

So that last evening, as we were getting ready to say our farewells, the vicar said 'we've actually prepared a little surprise for you', a sort of surprise farewell. And they piled me into their car, a Morris Minor, and we burbled around the island, to look for somewhere to go swimming. All the beaches on Ascension – which is basically a great big mid-ocean volcano – are made of black sand, except for one on the western side, which for some uncanny reason is pure white. So, armed with a picnic basket, we headed for this beach.

It was a full moon, brilliantly clear. The air was like velvet, and the sea flat as a mirror under the moonlight. We went down onto the beach and Nigel and Angela unpacked the picnic basket, which had a couple of bottles of good white wine – but also strawberries and cream, which the pair had picked up on the flight coming south from England, and which for them was an enormous treat. It was a treat for me as well, having been on a Russian ship for the previous two months, and just eating borsch and potatoes and rust.

So we sat on the beach under this ice-white, full moon and it was now maybe about 11 pm I suppose, we were eating strawberries and cream and swimming and thinking about how this was a really exceptional experience. But the vicar said, 'We've actually brought you here to see something.' He pointed out to sea. There was the white line of the surf crashing onto the beach in front and suddenly there were black shapes materializing in the surf, and great shapes, like soldiers coming up the beach at Dunkirk, crawling slowly towards us. It was a little strange, almost frightening; first 1 then 2 then 10 then 50, then 100 of these things making their way up the beach. I soon realized what they were: enormous Brazilian turtles that had swum all the way from near Recife to come and lay their eggs here on Ascension. And they turned around next to us at the high point of the beach and with their back flippers they, with tremendous exertion, carved little holes in the sand, and laid their clutches of eggs and then without a thought just motored back down into the sea and began swimming 2,500 miles all the way back, almost casually, as if they were shoppers going to Tesco. It was just extraordinary.

So I was watching this and marvelling and thinking this is the most wonderful evening – when suddenly it became extremely cold and we were all shivering. We couldn't work out why – until we looked up and saw that the moon was going into a total lunar eclipse. And then as that happened, out of the western horizon rose the Hale-Bopp comet, spectacularly beautiful, low on the horizon.

And it was at that precise moment that I began to think: I have not lived an especially virtuous life, yet here I am for some serendipitous reason being rewarded with new friends, strawberries, cream, cool white wine, swimming, turtles, an eclipse and a comet. It seemed all just too good to be true, this conjunction of wonderful things that seemed so very extraordinary.

And then the shadow of the earth moved away from the moon and the light returned. It became a little warmer, and the Hale-Bopp comet disappeared and then in its place were two very bright lights also on the south western horizon, which shone ever larger and became ever brighter, and of course turned out to be the RAF jet, which swept over our heads and landed with a screech – and suddenly it was time to go.

So we drove to the airport and the vicar and his wife put me on the plane and I said goodbye, and I thought back to what an extraordinary event that was. I woke at dawn. We got to Brize at about seven in the morning and I thought that as I was early for my flight to New York I would go into Oxford, where I was having a jacket made by my tailor there. So I went to the shop, and they were just opening and I said 'Is John the tailor there?' He was, and was surprised to see me. But he said 'Yes, come up to the fitting room; the jacket is ready to be fitted' or some such. So I went up and unrolled my shirtsleeves while standing on this beautiful parquet floor with a lovely rug on it and a blizzard of white sand cascaded out onto the floor. And John said, 'What's all that about?' And I said 'Well I've just been on a beach in Ascension Island', and told him the story that I have just related, and all the while he was patiently measuring and pinning. And then he took me downstairs. It was raining and he took me out into the street to walk off to the station to catch my train down to London. And he said 'That story is just the greatest episode of serendipity that I think I've ever heard.' And then I walked out into the rain and caught my train.

My life seems to have been punctuated by moments like this and I am enormously, without meaning to be unduly sentimental about it, grateful that these things have happened. But that, the episode in Ascension, which was essentially all about the kindness, the unexpected, unanticipated and serendipitous kindness of strangers that led to it, had no effect really on my career. It's just a story to tell, an event to remember. But the other events actually did direct my career in a very significant way and I want to try and tell you a few of those and to reiterate that I am in consequence enormously grateful to serendipity as a perpetual mechanism in my life.

I started life as a geologist. I went to Oxford and got a degree, but a degree that was staggeringly bad, which I put down to the myriad distractions that plagued Oxford in the 1960s. The degree was so bad that not only could I not contemplate doing research, but had to go into industry or trade, and indeed worse than that – trade in the colonies. I was sent to Uganda to go and look for copper, finding myself working for a Canadian company called Falconbridge of Africa.

So all of a sudden I found myself in western Uganda with a hammer and 25 Ugandans working for me, and living in a tiny, tented encampment in a place called Kyenjojo near Lake Albert. I was completely hopeless at my job: in my months there I didn't find a microgram of copper. But I was obsessed with mountain climbing, not least because my work had me exploring in the foothills of the Ruwenzori Mountains, on the border with Congo. The British Council back in those days had a library at a place called Fort Portal, and I would go there every week and get any book I could find on mountains to read in my tent in between not finding copper.

And one day entirely at random I took out a book called *Coronation Everest* published by Faber in London by a chap called James Morris. I read it in my tent that night and devoured it. James Morris was *The Times* correspondent on the successful expedition led by John Hunt, and on which the summit was reached by Tenzing Norgay and Edmund Hillary. James Morris had never climbed before in his life, yet managed to get to 23,000 feet. More than that, more than the story of the derring-do and the excitement of being on a remarkable climbing expedition, he was the one who managed, by a very subtle and cunning series of codes, to outwit all the other correspondents, the *Daily Mail* and the *Telegraph* particularly, in getting the news of the success of Hillary and Tenzing back to London in time to be published in *The Times* on the morning of the Queen's Coronation, on 2 June 1953.

And I remember as a small boy, as I daresay some readers will too, waking up that morning not merely to the realization that this new young Queen was being crowned, but also that a British expedition, in a final sort of Imperial hurrah, had managed to get to the summit of the world's highest mountain. And James Morris was the person who engineered that news being published in London.

I was completely captivated by the book, and so I wrote that night to James Morris care of his publishers, Faber & Faber, 3 Queen Square, London saying:

> Dear Mr Morris, I am a 21 year old geologist living in East Africa. I have just read your book and my basic question is – can I be you?

And you'd think he would ignore it but he didn't. Two weeks later came a reply, which I still have, saying:

> Dear Mr Winchester, I am so delighted that you read and enjoyed my book and my advice to you is quite simple. If you really think you can write and if you still want to, then on the very day you receive this letter, not tomorrow, not in a week's time, certainly not in a month's time, but the very day, march into your office there in Uganda, resign, come back to Britain, get a job on a local newspaper and write to me again.

So I did precisely that. The smiles of relief and delight on the faces of the managers were a sight to be seen, they were so pleased. A taxi took me to Entebbe courtesy of the company; they put me on the plane, BOAC, and waved goodbye. And I arrived ten hours later in a rainy, winter evening in London thinking: I'm 21 years old, I've got a degree from Oxford, admittedly a second, but still, and surely some newspaper somewhere will give me a job.

Well at first nobody hired me. They just did not want to know. And so for six months I worked on an oil rig in the North Sea, based in Lowestoft of all places. But still applying for newspapers and reading all of James' books – books on Oxford and on Spain and Venice – and realized that

I was dealing with – though I'd never heard of him before the Everest book – a real heavy hitter of a writer.

Eventually a newspaper in Newcastle-upon-Tyne hired me as a very junior reporter whereupon I wrote to James and said, 'all right, I am now a reporter as you suggested, in Newcastle-upon-Tyne, what now?' And in his reply you can sense the gulp of 'you took this advice?' But then he was very good about it because he then gave me three pieces of firm advice, which he said 'follow and you'll do all right':

1. Never lose your sense of wonder about the world. If you are a newspaper correspondent you are likely to get jaded or bored or cynical. Don't. You're in an unrivalled position to see an extraordinary part of humankind. Never cease to exhibit your wonder at it; it is a remarkable thing you've got.
2. Don't bother to learn shorthand. They'll tell you that you have to but ignore them, you just don't need it.
3. Every month package up the articles you are writing for the newspaper, send them to me – and he lived in a little village in North Wales called Llanystumdwy – and I will annotate them, send them back to you and hope that we can turn you into something of a reasonable writer.

And so that's exactly what I did – and you can imagine that in those early days the kind of stories one would write were really very minor, you know 'Four Nuns In Car Crash, None Hurt'; 'Pigeon Fancier Loses Prize Bird', that kind of thing. But I would send them to Llanystumdwy and back they would come from James with: this paragraph a little long, this sentence a little heavy, this verb a little infelicitously chosen – and slowly, very slowly I think, under his tutelage I became a better writer.

But we never met. Not at first, anyway.

After two and a half or so years he advised me to join the *Guardian*, and by great good fortune I managed to get a job there. And the *Guardian* sent me almost immediately to Belfast and I had, at the very beginning of the troubles, three very exciting years, with my writings all over the front page, and my career began to take off.

Then after three years in Belfast – and essentially as a reward for having survived it – the paper sent me to Washington, and I'd arrived just at the beginning of the Watergate scandal, so once again by great good fortune I was all over the front pages and life from a journalistic point of view was really sweet. And throughout all of this I was keeping in touch with James in Wales.

On 9 August 1974, Richard Nixon resigned the presidency and that obviously was a major story and then on 8 September – the day on which President Ford pardoned Richard Nixon – I somewhat incautiously chose to cover Evel Knievel's attempt to ride his motorcycle over the Snake River Canyon in Idaho. That story was not used and I was given something of a wigging. I decided to come back to Britain for a fortnight or so and go climbing, which I was still interested in doing.

Meanwhile, I had rung an Australian friend of mine on the paper, a young woman called Jackie Leishman, and asked her whether she would like to come to North Wales with me for a few days to go climbing. She said yes, and in the car on the way up she said 'Doesn't your friend James Morris live here?' (because everyone knew that James had created the monster that I had become in the paper). And I said 'Yes but I've never spoken to him, I've never met him.' And she said 'Well that's completely ridiculous, he'd be enormously proud, as soon as we get to the hotel', the Pen-y-Gwryd in Llanberis, 'we'll ring him up.' So we looked up the telephone number and she rang – I didn't really have the courage to do it – and she pressed the receiver to my ear, and there was this voice, and I said 'It's Simon Winchester' and this person said 'This is amazing, I mean I read you every morning from Washington, where are you?' And I said 'I'm in Llanberis about three miles away.' 'You must come for tea tomorrow' he said. And so it was settled, at 4 o'clock the next day we would motor down to Llanystumdwy and go and have tea.

So Jackie and I went climbing and came down from the hills in time to get to Llanystumdwy at tea time. We drove into the driveway of this extremely nice country house. It was something that I shall never forget. We parked the car and walked over to the front doorstep and you could see through the glass windows acres of polished floors and oriental carpets and we were filthy dirty because we'd been tramping around on our way up Tryfan. So I rang the doorbell and we were both kneeling down on the front step unlacing our climbing boots as the door opened and a woman appeared. I said 'Oh hello, I'm Simon Winchester and this is Jackie Leishman, you must be Mrs Morris.' And this person said 'No, I'm James actually.'

Well you can imagine, but this was the 1970s and people wore their hair fairly long and so, as cheerfully as I could, I said 'Oh well, you can never tell these days, I'm terribly sorry.' But then this person said 'I'll call my wife' and I thought, no hang on a minute. The Welsh are a peculiar people anyway but this is obviously some strange Celtic joke, because James had climbed Mount Everest to 20-odd thousand feet, had been a Captain in a brigade of guards, had fathered four children, had walked across the Hadramaut. He was very much a man's man, so clearly whoever was going to come down the stairs would be bearded with a Yukon Jack shirt or something. Not at all: along comes a middle-aged English lady with a little girl in tow, and we all trooped into the drawing room to have tea – with me fairly obviously a man, and Jackie my friend, fairly obviously a young woman and Elizabeth Morris, a middle-aged lady, and Suki, a little girl, and then my hero sitting there in a twin set and pearls, a little hanky tucked into her sleeve, tight tweed pencil skirt, little court shoes, legs decorously crossed, all the accoutrements – and very substantial accoutrements I might mention – of womanhood, all very visible.

But of course being British nothing was said about it. We just sat there and drank our tea and ate our Rich Tea biscuits and spoke of the weather and the crops. And then at about six-thirty or so we left and with Jackie, a forthright Australian, as soon as we'd cleared the property saying 'what the **** was all that about?' And of course I had not the foggiest idea – but the next morning a note was hand-delivered to the hotel saying:

> Dear Simon, I do apologise for putting you through what must have been a somewhat awkward social situation, but the fact of the matter is that I've decided to become a woman. I am going to Casablanca next week to have the necessary surgery and if it's successful I'll be reborn under the name Jan Morris and I hope that you can accept that and I hope that we'll be friends.

Well we've remained friends now for – that was in 1974 so that was 34 years ago. We've written a book together, we see each other all the time; we were in Shanghai and Hong Kong together last spring-time. I'd almost venture to say we're bosom buddies but I don't think that's quite the right phrase. (So people that would apply for the *Guardian* jobs would be told by the editor then in the 1970s: how do you get a job on the *Guardian*? Well you become a geologist and then you befriend a transsexual, and then you'll be absolutely fine.)

One of the things that Jan told me throughout was it was important to attempt to write books because newspaper stories, however wonderful they might be to research and however much fun they were to read in the paper, essentially wrapped fish and chips a couple of days later. They have little permanence about them. Books, however, are another matter. 'Try' she said 'every couple of years or every place you go to, to get a book out of whatever you're doing.'

And so I did. I've followed her advice essentially to the letter my entire career, though all the early books were stunningly unsuccessful. I mean, the first book was about Northern Ireland, which was written in the early 1970s, and it did no business at all. The second book, which celebrated the Bicentenary of the United States, was called *American Heartbeat*, the royalties – I mean royalty, that's a laugh! – it sold 11 copies. And book after book after book did dismally poorly. The advances came in, the books that resulted essentially made a seamless progress from my typewriter to the remainder table with the appearance in bookstores being a sort of gaudy irrelevance – they were hardly there for any time at all. The publishers were amazing, though, in that they continued to have some sort of faith. *Maybe you'll get it right next time*, they would say, and they would still hand out the advances and still the sales figures would be dismal, and that was the situation in 1997, about the time of the Hong Kong handover, which I was over to cover.

I had written a book that year on the Yangzi River, which like all the previous books had been relatively politely reviewed – but no one wanted to buy it. And yet once again my publishers, particularly my American publishers, had said, well let's give him one more chance, and they asked me, what did I want to write about next? I said I wanted to write a book which was a hymn to the practice of tramp shipping, that I wanted to buy an 800-ton tramp steamer and with a bunch of friends of mine sail it around the world to see if it could be done and so explore just what this dying way of maritime life was all about. And they advanced me the money to do it and, you know, I was very gung ho about the project. Maybe this book would be my breakout success?

Well there came a point towards the end of 1997 when my publisher in New York, a woman called Marian Wood, called me in for a meeting just to find out how the book was going, whether I'd bought the ship and when I would be setting sail and what the delivery date for the manuscript would be. So we had a lunch in New York and then went, as is customary, back to her office and she very proudly showed me – all editors do this – the books that she was publishing that autumn season. 'Take any book you want', she said. Somewhere on her shelf stood one book called *Chasing the Sun: Dictionaries and the Men Who Made Them* by a man called Jonathon Green. I had a copy of the *Oxford English Dictionary*, which I'd bought in Hong Kong and so I was sort of interested in dictionaries. My choice wasn't particularly profound; it may have been that the other books that Marian was publishing weren't hugely interesting.

At the time I had a little house in Upstate New York, about 150 miles north of New York City, and I read the book that night and I picked it up again the following morning. I was sufficiently enthralled by it that I decided to continue reading it in the bath. The book included a curious footnote which said 'readers of this book', obviously relatively specialist people, 'will of course be familiar, of course, with the story of W. C. Minor, the deranged American lunatic murderer who was such a prolific contributor to the *Oxford English Dictionary*'.

I must have sat up in the bath like Archimedes. There was something about that sentence, about a deranged American lunatic murderer, a contributor to the *OED*, that just sounded too good to be true. And here's the serendipitous moment. Beside the bath was a telephone and it was 12:15 in London, in Oxford, in Cambridge, 7:15 in the morning where I was having my bath and I just happened to remember the telephone number of the only lexicographer in the world I know, a woman called Elizabeth Knowles, in Oxford. I picked up the phone and with a dripping hand I dialled her number, which remains engraved on my heart to this day.

At first she didn't answer – and then finally, rather breathlessly, picked up the phone, slightly irritated. And I said 'Elizabeth, this is Simon, and first of all I want to tell you – and I hope you don't think it's vulgar – but I'm telephoning you from my bath in America. And I want to ask you: do you know anything about a chap called W. C. Minor?' And she said 'Well, you're jolly lucky: first of all I was just going out to lunch and

I heard the phone from down the corridor, and I came back to answer it, and yes, the answer to your question is I do, I probably know more about W. C. Minor than anyone on the planet.' Because it turns out that she had written an account of W. C. Minor and the impact he had on the structure of the *Oxford English Dictionary* for a lexicographical journal published in Madison, Wisconsin somewhat unimaginatively called *Dictionaries*. And if I would do her the honour, she said, of towelling myself dry and standing by the fax machine, she would fax it over to me.

So I stood there and these pages started coming through and all I was really interested in was to look at the bibliography at the end: *had there been a book already published?* Well there hadn't, so far as the list was concerned, and as I was feeling sort of cheerful about this she rang back and she said 'Oh, I just wanted to tell you that, as you may know, Minor was incarcerated for the better part of four decades at Broadmoor', a lunatic asylum outside London, 'and I was allowed in there once and I saw his medical records: eleven linear feet of papers. But I wasn't allowed to read them. I warrant that if you can get permission to read those papers there's a rather good story to be told.'

That morning I began a proposal saying 'I think there's a book here in the story of how a deranged American lunatic murderer was a principal contributor to the *OED*. I could do this book in a matter of weeks or months, provided I get permission to see the medical records, and it needn't delay the book on the ship. May I?'

The next morning my editor in London rang up and she said this was a terrific idea, you've got to do this book, but offered a sum of money so derisory, it essentially wasn't worth going out of the house for. So I consoled myself with 'don't worry, the Americans, they're a generous people, they will realise the importance of this story, they'll offer more'. Well, at 2 o'clock in the afternoon, Marian Wood, my editor of the tramp steamer book, rang to say 'you know, this isn't a book, this is a magazine article for the *New Yorker* or the *Smithsonian* or *Harper's*, but it's not a book. You've got to remember you're under contract to write a book about tramp steamers, so my advice to you is to forget this book and just move on with your life and just buy this ship and hurry up.'

And so the following February I was in London with a certified cheque for a considerable amount of money to buy the ship. I was staying at the

Travellers' Club on Pall Mall and had a lunchtime appointment to hand over the cheque. There was a terrific rain storm, making it difficult to get a taxi. I was just about to go down in the rain to get it when Albert, the doorman, said 'Oh, Mr Winchester there's a telephone call for you' and I said 'Albert, I can't take the call, I've got a cab, they're very hard to get today.' He said 'No, no you don't understand, it's a call from America.' I somehow would have felt that the switchboard operator at the Travellers' Club would be relatively sophisticated about calls from the States. To him, however, this was clearly a momentous event and so I said 'Okay Albert, I'll take the call.'

On the other end of the line was Larry Ashmead, an editor at Harper-Collins. He'd been walking through the offices of Penguin Books in London the previous week looking for book ideas to buy and had seen on the edge of someone's desk a proposal for a book about the *Oxford English Dictionary* and the involvement of an American murderer. And he said to the editor, 'What is that?' And she said 'Oh, I'm just actually ... it's on the right-hand side of the desk because I'm just throwing it in the garbage because the Americans don't want it and Simon Winchester isn't going to write it.' He said 'Let me read it and take it back to New York.'

He had called to tell me he was willing to offer serious money for it. I went to lunch, did not hand the cheque to the ship's owner but, instead, came back and I called my editor in New York, Marian Wood. I explained the situation and asked her what I should do. She replied that the first thing to do is to read the small print on my contract: *You are not permitted to write any book about any other subject for any publisher until you've finished this one.* 'You have never written a book about history, you've never written a book about lexicography, you are a travel writer, and my advice to you is to stick to your last because if you decide to write this book and we decide to negate the contract we will demand every penny piece back that we have paid you already.'

That weekend was agonizing. Most of my friends told me to me go for it. Their basic advice held that I had been so spectacularly unsuccessful so far, how much worse could life get? So on Monday I rang Larry and said I would do the book on the dictionary for him, and I rang Marian to say that I would not do the book on ships. (Within ten minutes the lawyers from her publishing firm were on the line demanding the money back.)

More relevant are the serendipitous events leading up to the book's eventual success. Who would have thought, after all, that a book on lexicography, an arid subject above all else, would actually sell at all, let alone sell well? It was published in Britain and did tolerably well: it had nice reviews and was due out in America in six months. Once you've finished a book on a particular subject you leave the editors and people to deal with it and you get on with the next subject – the next subject for me being on the Arctic (it actually turned out that I didn't write the book). To research it I had to travel way up to Northern Canada, to the very farthest tip of Ellesmere Island, sledding in the wake of an expedition by a man called Greely that had first been undertaken 100 years earlier.

The Canadian Government demands that up in their Arctic you take a radio. Rifles aren't permitted, which is annoying because there are polar bears all over the place. But at least we had access to a radio. One day in late April there was a call for a 'Simon Winchester'. I took the call. They wondered whether I was anywhere near a telephone. I said 'No, I mean I think there's a geological field camp about 100 miles away that's got a radio telephone.' 'Well, if you can get to a telephone there's someone in New York that wants to speak to you urgently.' So I said 'All right.'

We changed the direction of the expedition and sledded towards this geological field camp and sure enough there was a touch-tone telephone, and a New York number. On the other end of the line was a woman called Jane Beirn who introduced herself as my publicist. Now I'd never had a publicist in my entire career, I didn't know what publicists did; none of my books merited a publicist. Well, she said 'We have had a request from the *New York Times* to talk to you about your new book about the dictionary' and in this business if the *New York Times* says jump basically you say *how high?* 'So are you anywhere near an airstrip?' they asked. And I said 'Well, there is one about 50 miles further on', and she said 'Can you go there? We'll pay, we'll send a plane, get yourself down to New York. He wants to have lunch with you on Thursday.'

So we changed direction yet again, found the airstrip, a De Havilland Twin Otter came in and picked me up, took me via Resolute to Ottawa, and on to New York. There, in an Italian restaurant in the Upper West Side, I met Mel Gussow, responsible for a column called 'At Lunch

With . . .' and featuring basically anyone he fancied as moderately interesting and appropriate for the arts section of the *Times*.

So we talked for two and a half hours, a photographer came along and took my picture, and I rejoined my friend in Resolute. We completed the expedition and flew back to New York on schedule. Back home I rang the publicist and I said 'What was all that about?' She said 'Well, Mel Gussow is this enormously well respected writer and any piece by him is well worth having in terms of publicity.' 'He rang me', she continued, 'to say he loved the interview, everything went swimmingly, and it will appear he promised on a Monday, and with any luck on the front page of the arts section.'

Well, all the Mondays in May went past: nothing appeared. All the Mondays in June did too, and those in July, and those in August. And then at the very end of August Jane rang and said 'I have some good news and some bad news. The good news is that the piece on your book on the *Oxford English Dictionary* appears on the front page of the *New York Times* on Monday and it's a wonderful piece. Mel Gussow loved the book and there are five photographs. The bad news, however, is that next Monday in America – and as an Englishman you may not know this – it is Labour Day, and no one in New York, believe me *no one*, reads that day's *New York Times*.'

Well as it happened on Labour Day in New York in 1998 it rained. All day. And New Yorkers sitting in their cabanas and on their beach houses in the Hamptons had nothing to do *but* read the *New York Times*. They may not have ventured out to their Barnes & Nobles and Borders stores, but they did go online, with the result that that night the book got to Number One on Amazon.com. So there you have it: a classic example of serendipity (in the rain).

It changed my life. That book propelled me from a totally unsuccessful author to someone who was at last turning a writing life into a living. It's an extraordinary fortunate situation to be in and I'm keenly aware of how extraordinarily lucky I am that the succeeding books have all, for one reason or another, done moderately well.

The most recent of these books brought me to Cambridge to write about this extraordinary character Joseph Needham. Born in 1900, he was the son of a doctor and an extraordinarily volatile musician. He went up to Gonville & Caius College, Cambridge, and became a biochemist, specializing in the egg, and married a woman called Dorothy. He was many extraordinary things: a chain smoker, a nudist, an accordion player, a Morris dancer, an ardent Marxist.

Life should have progressed in a seamless sort of way. They should have been typical left wing, Cambridge academics, had it not been for the arrival of a young Chinese female student, Lu Gwei-Djen, in 1937. They fell in love. It is a beautiful story and I won't go into it in any great detail but suffice to say that from 1938 onwards she, Lu Gwei-Djen, taught Joseph Chinese. He read and wrote it with great facility; spoke it with less facility but well. The British Government sent him on an official mission to China in 1942, whereupon he conceived the idea of writing a book about the history of Chinese Science, which by the time he died in 1995 had evolved into the longest, most massive piece of scholarship in the English language on China. Comprising 24 volumes, it is essentially all by the hand of this one remarkable and really rather undeservedly obscure Cambridge man.

My hope is that this book will lift him from obscurity, at least in our part of the world. For in China, every school child knows the name Li Yue-se – his Chinese name. In fact, I had an extraordinary illustration of this not many years ago. At the time – December 2006 – my wife had an apartment in Washington DC and worked for National Public Radio. On this particular evening she was working on an urgent project that didn't allow us either to go out for dinner, or to cook, that night. So we decided to send out for Chinese food. We rang Mr Chen's Organic Chinese Restaurant, ordered some food, and we were told it would be 45 minutes. And sure enough 45 minutes later, the doorbell announced the arrival of a Chinese courier with two plastic bags. However, when the moment came to pay, we realized that neither of us had any cash on us. Well, we had $8 and I think the bill was $40. So he said, 'Don't worry, there's an ATM down in the street', so I said to my wife 'Okay, you lay the table and I'll be back in a couple of minutes.'

So this chap and I went to the lift, I pressed the button and it didn't come. I was whistling tunelessly and tapping my fingers on the dado and eventually said to this chap, 'Where are you from?' And he said 'Shanghai' and I said 'Oh yes, I know a little bit about Shanghai' and we talked a bit about where exactly. Just to make conversation, I told him about the book I was writing. He looked about as interested as a Chinese delivery man would at this utterly irrelevant piece of information. But then I said 'Li Yue-se' and he suddenly came alive and animated. 'You're writing a book about Li Yue-se?', and I said 'You know him?', and he said 'Know him? – Of course! He's the most famous Englishman that ever lived in China, everyone knows Li Yue-se.' I said 'Well, that's absolutely wonderful, would you like to see some photographs and original letters that I have back in the flat?'

And so we went back into the apartment where my wife was just getting ready to chow down and here I was back with the delivery guy, and I said 'This man knows Li Yue-se, let's show him some pictures.' And so we showed him some of our things to which he responded with polite interest. Ten or so minutes later, my wife whispered: 'Actually I think he's probably wanting his money, I think he's probably being polite, why don't you . . .' so I said 'Yes, of course.'

We made our way to the ATM and I gave him his money, and the customary tip, said goodbye and walked back to the apartment. As I did so I heard footsteps behind. I looked around and it was him, still there. Obviously he'd parked his bike or his car or whatever was his mode of transport near the doorway to the apartment and although I'd officially finished the conversation, as it were, it seemed churlish not to continue. So I said 'When you lived in Shanghai what was your job?' And he said 'Oh, I used to work in the computer department of the Standard Chartered Bank.' And because I knew this one tiny little nugget of trivial information that Standard Charter in Shanghai used to be called McCauley's Bank and is known as Macally Bank I said to him 'Oh, Macally Bank' – and he stopped dead still in the middle of Columbia Road and cocked his head to one side and said 'Simon?' And I looked at him, and said 'Gordon?'

It turned out that I had made a film about this very man 20 years before. We had been making a series of films on the last ten years of Imperial Hong Kong and one of the things we did was to film a Standard Chartered Banker in Hong Kong. He was everything one would have imagined him to be: young and upwardly mobile with a BMW and flat in Repulse Bay, and a girlfriend that looked like a model, and holidays in Thailand. We contrasted him with this guy called Gordon Cui,

Cui Guo-hong from Shanghai (our delivery man), who lived in a fifth floor walk-up, filthy with coal dust, and ate not much more than rice and white cabbage while his wife worked in a factory assembling radios. The general idea was to see how their lives might slowly converge as the ten final years of Hong Kong as a colony unrolled.

So we filmed him in 1987 and again in 1988. In fact, I flew him down to Hong Kong to meet his counterpart. Then, a year later he told me that he wanted more than anything to go to the United States and pursue a Ph.D. at Drexel University in Philadelphia. And so I sponsored his visa application and paid his first semester's tuition at Drexel and he went, as far as I knew, and then completely dropped out of sight. The next time I met him was in New York City, carrying two bags of imperial purple rice up to our apartment.

I should perhaps tell you the coda to it, I mean I took him back to the apartment as you can imagine with my wife going completely mad, I mean she just wanted to eat her dinner and yet here I was bringing the delivery guy back again. Anyway, he then took us out to dinner, he was overjoyed, I mean both of us were incredibly moved by this extraordinary coincidence – this serendipitous occurrence. And he told us that he had indeed got his PhD and had subsequently joined General Motors of Canada as its Government was fast tracking Chinese applicants for visas, and he thusly become a Canadian citizen. Then, in 1999, he had returned to the United States to work on a secret communications protocol for the Raytheon Corporation but, along with all non-American employees, had lost his job after 9/11. However, given his qualifications, he was able to set up as a consultant. He would consult all day before collecting his wife from work at six o'clock, drop her off at home, and drive down to his friend and restaurateur Mr Chen. There he'd park himself outside the restaurant to read technical manuals, while Mr Chen, every so often, would ask him to deliver a couple of plastic bags to a local address. And so he began making deliveries while preparing for the next day's consulting assignment.

In concluding, I do not wish to become overly philosophical about the nature of serendipity except in suggesting that it changed my life in profound ways. Why did I remember that telephone number, pick up the telephone and call Elizabeth Knowles? Why did it rain on that particular day? How did Cui Guo-hong come back into my life all those years later? Why did those extraordinary things happen on Ascension Island? Of course I can't answer any of these questions conclusively. However, I do think that some people have, if you like, a prepared mind – there is some sort of openness, a willingness to accept and hope and be optimistic that makes them particular candidates for serendipitous occurrences. I cannot be any more profound than that, but some people, including myself, have been blessed by this extraordinary way that serendipitous occurrences just seem magnetically to stick to me and I am extraordinarily delighted for it.

I want to finish by telling you the one small but remarkable thing that happened to me just ten days ago in Sri Lanka where, as you well know, the concept of serendipity was born. There is a large mountain in Sri Lanka's central southern part called Adam's Peak, so named because some people think that's where Adam stepped on the Earth first. On top of it lies a big footprint and a temple revered by many religions, principally nowadays the Buddhists.

I figured I might like to climb the mountain to watch the sun rise from atop its peak. So I left the base at about one o'clock in the morning to clamber through the clouds for four hours. All that remains is to wait for the sun to rise. It was a bitterly cold but beautiful morning – as the light started to come up in the east, you could see the mist in the valleys and all the tea plantations around you, and in the far distance Colombo and then Galle to the south and the Indian Ocean a long, long way off. And it was utterly, utterly beautiful.

So I went to this tiny little temple at the very, very summit of this extraordinary mountain and saw in gold and filigree the Buddha's footprint and I was just climbing down from it when I heard a voice which said, 'Simon?' And I turned around and there was a man who I last saw at Tiger Leaping Gorge in China in 1988, called Geoff Naylor. And we were amazed at seeing one another and we shook hands and we walked down the mountain together and went and had breakfast. And both of us said to one another, 'You know that's serendipity.'

Notes on the contributors

Mark de Rond is a reader at the Judge Business School and a Fellow of Darwin College, Cambridge, with a particular interest in causation, explanation and imaginations of human importance in organizational life. His published work has received several prestigious awards, including the George R. Terry Book Award and inclusion in the Best of Books 2008 (*Financial Times*).

Iain Morley is a Fellow of Keble College, Oxford, where he is Tutor in Archaeology and Anthropology, and a lecturer for the Institute of Human Sciences. A scholar of archaeology and the evolution of human cognition, he has undertaken archaeological fieldwork around the world, and has published books and articles on the origins of music, early ritual and religion. He was formerly a Research Fellow of Darwin College.

Susan Alcock is Professor of Classics at Brown University, Joukowsky Family Professor of Archaeology, and Director of the Artemis A. W. and Martha Sharp Joukowsky Institute for Archaeology and the Ancient World. She has directed several archaeological fieldwork projects and is the author or editor of ten books on the Greek and Roman world, including *Archaeologies of the Greek Past: Landscapes, Monuments and Memories* (2001), which won the Spiro Kostof Award from the Society of Architectural Historians.

Richard Leakey has been responsible for some of the most significant discoveries in the study of human origins and evolution, as well as being a major contributor to conservation and politics in Kenya. He has been Director of the National Museums of Kenya, Director of Kenya Wildlife Service, Permanent Secretary, Secretary to the Cabinet, and Head of the Civil Service of Kenya. He is currently Chairman of the Turkana Basin Institute and Professor of Anthropology at the State University of New York, Stony Brook.

Robin A. Weiss is Professor of Viral Oncology at University College London. He has spent most of his career studying retroviruses, contributing to the discovery of viral genomes inherited as Mendelian traits in host DNA. He is currently President of the Society for General Microbiology and in 2007 was awarded the prestigious Ernst Chain Award by Imperial College, in recognition of his pioneering work on understanding HIV and AIDS, and AIDS-associated malignancies.

Simon Singh is a well-known science author and BBC television presenter. He has been a producer and director for BBC TV, working on programmes such as *Tomorrow's World* and *Horizon*, and won a BAFTA for his documentary about Fermat's Last Theorem. His best-selling books include *Fermat's Last Theorem*, *The Code Book*, *Big Bang* and *Trick or Treatment? Alternative Medicine on Trial*. He holds a Ph.D. in particle physics from Cambridge University.

Andy Fabian FRAS FRS OBE is a Royal Society research professor at the Institute of Astronomy at the University of Cambridge, Vice-Master of Darwin College and President of the Royal Astronomical Society. His research focuses in particular on X-ray astronomy, black holes, active galactic nuclei and clusters of galaxies. He was awarded the American Astronomical Society's Bruno Rossi Prize in 2001, and was made an Officer of the Order of the British Empire (OBE) in 2006.

Sir Richard Friend FREng FRS is Cavendish Professor at the University of Cambridge and a Fellow of St John's College. He is known throughout the world for his ground-breaking work on the physics and engineering of carbon-based semiconductors, and co-founded Cambridge Display Technologies Ltd and Plastic Logic Ltd. He was awarded the IEE's Faraday Medal and was knighted in 2003.

Oliver Letwin MP FRSA is Member of Parliament for Dorset West, a member of the Privy Council and a Minister in the Coalition Government. He was formerly a Research Fellow of Darwin College and holds a Ph.D. from Trinity College, Cambridge. He has published numerous articles and books, including *Ethics, Emotion and the Unity of the Self* (1984), *Privatising the World* (1987), *Aims of Schooling* (1988), *Drift to Union* (1990) and *The Purpose of Politics* (1999).

Simon Winchester FRGS OBE is a writer and regular contributor to magazines and newspapers including *National Geographic* and *Condé Nast Traveller.* He has been a foreign correspondent for the *Guardian* and *The Sunday Times,* and is the author of over sixteen books, including *The Surgeon of Crowthorne* (1998), *The Map That Changed the World* (2001) and *The Man Who Loved China* (2008). He was made an Officer of the Order of the British Empire in 2006.

Index

AIDS *see* HIV
Alpher, Ralph 70–1
anthropology 27–43
  chances of a fossil being discovered
    29–30
  chances of a human ancestor being
    fossilized 28–9
  discovery of early hominids 31–6
  effects of climate change 41–2
  exploiting opportunities 31–6
  hominid brain enlargement 39–40
  language and communication 42
  no conscious choice in evolution 27–8,
    30–1
  origin and implications of bipedalism
    8–9, 36–40
  recognizing accidental opportunities
    31–6
  rise of modern humans 40–1
  role of serendipity in evolution 36–40
  search for human origins 31–6
  unanticipated benefits of adaptations
    30–1, 36–40
archaeology
  long-term operation of serendipity
    20–1
  radiocarbon dating 18
  regional survey 18–20
  reinterpretation of earlier discoveries
    20–1
  role of luck 16–17
  serendipity pattern 17–20
  tendency to deny serendipity 21–2
  use of spy satellite imagery 20

Archimedes 14–15, 16
astronomy 73–88
  black holes 77, 80, 81–3
  Comet Holmes 77–8
  Crab Nebula 78–9
  data volume management challenges
    81
  discoveries by amateurs 77–8
  extrasolar planets 83–6
  gamma-ray bursts 80–1
  gravitational lensing 82
  magnetars 80–1
  mapping the visible sky 81
  neutron stars 77, 78–9, 80–1
  prediction of phenomena 81
  pulsars 67–8, 78–9, 80–1
  research approaches and priorities 77,
    86–8
  ripples in gas at the centre of a cluster
    82–3
  search for extraterrestrial intelligence
    86
  supernovae 78–9, 80
  volcanoes of Io 73
  X-ray astronomy 77
Australopithecus 8–9

Barber, Elinor 13, 14, 16
bats, infections emanating from 55–6
Bell, Jocelyn 67–8, 78–9
Bernard, Claude 2
Big Bang model 68–72
Binford, Lewis 17, 22
bipedalism 8, 36–40

Index

Black Death 52–3
black holes 77, 80, 81–3
Bose particles (bosons) 95–6, 98–9
Bott, David 105
bovine spongiform encephalitis (mad cow
    disease) 55
Bridgman, Percy 2
Burn, Paul 93
Burroughes, Jeremy 93

Cambridge Display Technology 95, 104
carbon-14 dating 18
carbon-based electronics 91–5
Carter, Howard 17
cataract operations 67
CCR5Δ32 mutation, and HIV risk 47
cervical cancer 48, 62
Chagas' disease 54
chicken-pox 49
cholera 51
Churchill, Winston 72
classical civilizations
    concepts of fortune 14
    impediments to serendipity 14–16
climate change, and human evolution
    41–2
Comet Holmes 78
cosmic microwave background (CMB)
    radiation 68–72
cosmology 65–72
    Big Bang model 68–72
    cosmic microwave background (CMB)
        radiation 68–72
    detection of galactic radio emissions
        65–6
    detection of radio signals from meteors
        68
    detection of solar radio waves 68
    discovery of pulsars 67–8
    origins of radio astronomy
        65–6
Crab Nebula 78–9
Creutzfeldt-Jakob Disease 55
Crick, Francis 2
cytomegalovirus 48, 62

Darwin, Charles 28, 32, 54, 59
Dawkins, Richard 28
de Mestral, George 66
de Montaigne, Michel 2
Dewar, James 97–8
Dirac, Paul 101–2
Discovery Space 76
Drake's equation 86
Duffy antigen status, and HIV risk 47–8

E. Coli O157 51–2
Ebola virus 56
eccentricity 116, 118
Eddington, Arthur 82
environmental change, and infectious
    disease 55–6
Eureka! moments 14–15, 16, 76, 91
European Convention on Human Rights
    117
evolution 27–43
    chances of a fossil being discovered
        29–30
    chances of a human ancestor being
        fossilized 28–9
    discovery of early hominids 8–9,
        31–6
    effects of climate change 41–2
    hominid brain enlargement 39–40
    language and communication 42
    no conscious choice in 27–8, 30–1
    origin and implications of bipedalism
        8–9, 36–40
    rise of modern humans 40–1
    role of serendipity 36–40
    search for human origins 31–6
    unanticipated benefits of adaptations
        30–1, 36–40
extrasolar planets 83–6
extraterrestrial intelligence, search for
    86

Feast, Jim 92
Fermi particles (fermions) 99
Fleming, Alexander 2, 45
Fortuna 14

Index

fossil record
  chances of a fossil being discovered
    29–30
  chances of a human ancestor being
    fossilized 28–9
  discovery of early hominids 8–9,
    31–6
Fractional Quantum Hall Effect 97
frameworks of incentives for
    citizen-reaction 114–18
Fry, Art 66–7
future of serendipity 22–3

galactic radio emissions 65–6
Galileo 97
gamma-ray bursts 80–1
Gamow, George 70
Garden of Eden (Sri Lanka, Serendip)
    3–4, 48
genital herpes 62
Giacconi, Ricardo 77
Google references to serendipity 11–12
Gosse, Philip 48
government action
  uncertainty of citizen-reaction 109–21
  unintended consequences 111–12
gravitational lensing 82
Greeks, concept of fortune 14

Harwit, Martin 2
Hendra virus 56
hermaion 14, 17
Herman, Robert 70–1
Hermes 14
Hewish, Anthony 78–9
Hey, Stanley 68
Higgs boson 95–6
Hill, Andrew 8
HIV
  anti-retroviral drug resistance 48
  first infection of a human 51
  interactions with other infections 62
  opportunistic infections in AIDS
    patients 62
  origins of 56–9

SIVcpz precursor virus 57–9
  social and economic impact of AIDS 61
  susceptibility to TB infection 62
  transfer from chimpanzees to humans
    56–9
HIV infection risk
  CCR5Δ32 mutation 47
  Duffy antigen status 47–8
Holmes, Andrew 93
Hooke, Robert 2
human evolutionary origins 27–43
  Australopithecus 8
  chances of a fossil being discovered
    29–30
  chances of a human ancestor being
    fossilized 28–9
  discovery of early hominids 8–9, 31–6
  effects of climate change 41–2
  hominid brain enlargement 39–40
  language and communication 42
  no conscious choice in evolution 27–8,
    30–1
  origin and implications of bipedalism
    8–9, 36–40
  rise of modern humans 40–1
  role of serendipity 36–40
  search for 31–6
  unanticipated benefits of adaptations
    30–1, 36–40
human rights 116–18

illiberal tendencies in politics 112–14
immunization against infectious disease
    62
infectious disease 45–63
  annual mortality caused by 62
  drug resistance in microbes 48
  emergence of new diseases 52–4
  forecasting emerging infections 55–6
  genetic resistance 46–7
  genetic susceptibility 47–8
  globalization of human infections 52–4
  history of transport and spread 52–4
  host and microbe evolutionary dynamics
    46–8

infectious disease (*cont.*)
    immune system evolution 46–8
    immunization 62
    impact today 61–2
    infections emanating from bats 55–6
    microbes 45–6
    origins of HIV 56–9
    provenance of human infections 48–52
    synergism between infections 62
    vaccination 62
influenza virus 50, 51
information access, open network society
        118–20
Io, volcanoes on 73

Jansky, Karl 65–6
Josephson, Brian 101–2

Kaposi's sarcoma virus 62

Large Hadron Collider 95–6
Leakey, Mary 8–9
legionnaires' disease 51
Libby, Willard 18
liberalism
    allowance for eccentricity 116, 118
    alternatives to legal enforcement
        114–18
    and human rights 116–18
    and uncertainty of citizen-reaction
        109–21
    benevolent liberalism vs. benevolent
        authoritarianism 120–1
    effects of wider access to information
        118–20
    essential characteristics of liberalism
        116–18
    frameworks of incentives for
        citizen-reaction 114–18
    illiberal tendencies in politics 112–14
    in the post-bureaucratic age 118–20
    incentives to bring about social goods
        114–18
    individual and group rights 116–18
    open network society 118–20

lice
    co-evolution with hosts 59–61
    indicators of human biology and
        evolution 59–61
    transmission of typhus 61
Lloyd, Geoffrey 15–16
Lyme disease 51–2

mad cow disease (bovine spongiform
        encephalitis) 55
magnetars 80–1
magnetic resonance imaging (MRI)
        systems 98, 101
malaria resistance 46–7
measles virus 50, 53
medical serendipity 67
Merton, Robert 13, 14, 16, 17, 19
meteors, radio signals from 68
Moore's Law 91
Morabito, Linda 73
mumps 53

neutron stars 77, 78–9, 80–1
Nipah virus 55–6

Onnes, Kamerlingh 98
open network society 118–20
organic light-emitting diodes 91, 93–5,
        104–5
Ötzi the Iceman 17

papilloma virus 48–9, 62
Pasteur, Louis 45, 72, 73
penicillin, discovery of 2, 45
Penzias, Arno 68–72
physics 91–107
    carbon-based electronics 91–5
    cuprate high temperature
        superconductors 99–100
    discovery of superconductivity
        97–9
    Eureka! moment 91
    importance of serendipity in research
        95–6
    materials physics 96

organic light-emitting diodes 91, 93–5,
104–5
polyacetylene field effect transistors
92–3
polymeric light-emitting diodes 91,
93–5, 104–5
superconductivity in metals 96, 97–101
physics research and serendipity 96–107
avoid working in a crowded field 100–1
cautions about the scientific literature
102–4
cautions about theory 101–2
funding outlier projects 105–6
look for technology outside the field
97–100
materials and process engineering
capabilities 104–5
Piltdown 'fossil hominid' hoax 32
Plastic Logic Ltd 105
political outlook, and response to
uncertainty 109–21
polyacetylene field effect transistors 92–3
polymeric light-emitting diodes 91, 93–5,
104–5
poly(phenylenevinylene), PPV 93–5
post-bureaucratic age in politics 118–20
Post-it notes 66–7
prehistoric Europe 18
preparedness, aim and luck 75
Priestley, Joseph 2
pulsars 67–8, 78–9, 80–1

Quantum Hall Effect 97

rabies 49–50
radio astronomy
cosmic microwave background (CMB)
radiation 68–72
detection of radio signals from meteors
68
detection of solar radio waves 68
discovery of pulsars 67–8
origins of 65–6
radiocarbon dating 18
Rayleigh, Lord 97

regional survey archaeology 18–20
Richet, Charles 2
Ridley, Harold 67
Romans, concept of fortune 14
Röntgen, Wilhelm Conrad 77
Root-Berstein, Robert 2
Ryan, Alan 117

SARS coronavirus 50, 52, 56
Schliemann, Heinrich 20–1
scientific serendipity 66–7
semiconductors, polymeric light-emitting
diodes 91, 93–5, 104–5
Serendip (Sri Lanka, Garden of Eden)
3–4, 48
serendipity
adoption and diffusion of the term
11–12
as accident and sagacity 12–13
as lucky coincidence 12
breakthrough innovations credited to
1–2
characteristics 73–7
definitions 12–13, 66
difficulty of definition 2–4
history and etymology 2–4
identification of 'magic moments' 7–8
origin of the term 11
popularity of the concept 1, 7–8
popularity of the term 11–12
possibilities for the prepared mind
123–41
role in the process of discovery 1–2
'serendipity lite' 12
'serendipity strong' 13
SIVcpz, HIV precursor virus 56–9
smallpox 50–1, 53–4, 62
Snow, John 51
solar radio waves 68
Spanish flu pandemic 51
spy satellite imagery, archaeological
information 20
Sri Lanka (Serendip) 3–4
Stigler's law of eponyms 77
Stonehenge 18

stratigraphy of serendipity 11–23
superconductivity in metals 96, 97–101
supernovae 78–9, 80
syphilis 53, 62

terracotta army of the First Emperor 17
Thomson, J. J. 97
Three Princes of Serendip tale 3–4, 12–13,
    14
time lag for serendipity to occur 16, 20–1
Tut-Ankh-Amun's tomb 17
Tyche 14
typhus transmission by lice 61

uncertainty, effect on political outlook
    109–21

vaccination 62
varicella-zoster virus 49

Velcro 66
Viagra 67
viruses, evolutionary relationships 48–9
volcanoes of Io 73

Walpole, Horace 3–4, 11, 12–13, 14, 16
Watson, James 2
Weil's disease 51–2
Wilson, Robert 68–72
writing life, openness to the possibility of
    serendipity 123–41

X-ray astronomy 77
X-ray Background (XRB) 77
X-rays, discovery of 77

Yersinia pestis (plague bacillus) 52–3

zoonoses 49–50, 51–2